WATCHING AMERICA'S DOOR

A TWENTIETH CENTURY FUND REPORT

WATCHING AMERICA'S DOOR

The Immigration Backlash and the New Policy Debate

Roberto Suro

1996 ◆ The Twentieth Century Fund Press ◆ New York

The Twentieth Century Fund sponsors and supervises timely analyses of economic policy, foreign affairs, and domestic political issues. Not-for-profit and nonpartisan, the Fund was founded in 1919 and endowed by Edward A. Filene.

Library of Congress Cataloging-in-Publication Data

Suro, Roberto.
    Watching America's door : the immigration backlash and the new
    policy debate / Roberto Suro.
            p.   cm.
    "A twentieth century fund report."
    Includes bibliographical references and index.
    ISBN 0-87078-383-1
    1. United States--Emigration and immigration--Government policy.
I. Title.
JV6483.S87   1996
325.79--dc20   96-30397
                                                                        CIP

Cover design and illustration: Claude Goodwin
Manufactured in the United States of America.

FOREWORD

There are, perhaps, only a handful of truly special qualities that define the American experiment. One can imagine a spirited argument among scholars about what these qualities might be—with one exception. It is impossible to imagine a serious discussion of the subject that does not begin with the premise that our history is special because we are a nation of immigrants. Moreover, at every stage of its development, the United States has embraced more diversity in terms of immigration than has any other place on earth. As the flow of people from one region has dried up or been cut off, a new area has opened up. Sometimes there have been gaps, often there has been confusion about what was actually going on, but one thing has remained consistent: at most stages in our history the vast bulk of immigration has been from a few locations.

Whenever immigration has been substantial—regardless of where the immigrants came from or where they congregated—the political reaction has been predictable. "Newcomers don't fit." "They detract from the quality of life." "They cost money and they will ultimately change the nation in undesirable ways." The fact that this has never turned out to be true has never stopped the issue from becoming part of the political debate of the moment. People live in the here and now, and the arrival of large numbers of immigrants means changes that take place almost as soon as the first waves of a given immigration appear on our shores.

Nothing, of course, has quite the immediacy of campaigns and elections. A few weeks can change everything. A few years normally alters the balance of political forces completely. In this context, immigration is bound to be a hot-button issue. Anywhere immigrants arrive in any numbers, the immigration issue becomes a part of the political agenda. And that is certainly the case in several parts of the United States today, most obviously in the nation's largest state, California.

In 1994, in fact, 59 percent of California voters approved Proposition 187, which aims at prohibiting illegal immigrants from receiving social or welfare services, bans them from public schools and universities, and prevents them from receiving publicly funded health care except in emergencies. Although federal and state restraining orders and ongoing legal challenges have prevented Proposition 187 from being enacted, the vote provides a stark indication of the depth of anti-immigrant sentiment in California.

In this context, the Twentieth Century Fund asked Roberto Suro, deputy national editor of the *Washington Post*, to revisit his 1995 Fund paper, *Remembering the American Dream*, and report on recent trends in immigration and on the contemporary political debate about how to handle them.

In that earlier work, Suro emphasized the great recent surge in immigration, which reached levels not seen since the turn of the century. He reflected upon the widespread uncertainty about what to make of the latest immigrants: Will the benefits of having them here outweigh the costs? Will they assimilate and become more like "us"? Does their presence aid or hurt in economic competition, a process now perceived by most citizens as a dog-eat-dog international struggle?

In this volume, Suro updates and elaborates on the information he presented about contemporary immigration in *Remembering the American Dream*. In addition, he carefully examines the political reactions at the grass-roots level to immigration. But his policy discussion is even broader in scope. He argues that the sweeping immigration bills of the past, designed to guide U.S. policy for decades at a time, have proven woefully ineffective and calls for a new national immigration policy—one that is more responsive. Washington should be prepared to adjust its priorities regularly, and shift resources in response to new needs at home and changes in the immigration flow from abroad. The question is not one of keeping people out, but rather shaping the flow so it meets our needs in a changing global economy.

Over the years, the Twentieth Century Fund has published a number of works that deal with immigration, including Thomas Muller's *Immigrants and the American City*, Alan Dowty's *Closed Borders*, and Gil Loescher's *Beyond Charity*. At present, Saskia Sassen is writing a book for the Fund exploring immigration and the world economy.

With this monograph, Suro expands and deepens his discussion and our understanding of the continuing debate about large-scale immigration in United States. On behalf of the Trustees of the Twentieth Century Fund, I thank him for this contribution.

Richard C. Leone, *President*
The Twentieth Century Fund
July 1996

CONTENTS

CHAPTER 1

WASHINGTON TAKES NOTICE

On a visit to an Orange County social services center in 1992, Barbara Coe became frightened by the changes immigration had brought to California. "I walked into this monstrous room full of people, babies, and little children all over the place, and I realized nobody was speaking English," recalls Coe. There is no outrage in her voice. She is a sixty-year-old grandmother quite certain she is describing events that simply defy common sense. "I was overwhelmed with this feeling: 'Where am I? What's happened here? Is this still the United States of America?'"[1]

On election day in November 1994, when the Proposition 187 ballot initiative to combat illegal immigration drew more votes than any candidate on any ballot anywhere in the country, Coe found that 4.6 million Californians shared her fears.

For three decades, since the abolition of the national quotas system of immigration controls in 1965, federal policies had accepted—even encouraged—steadily increasing levels of legal immigration and had taken few effective measures against the illegal influx. The United States reached a turning point, beginning in 1993, with the controversy over the employment of an illegal alien that sank Zoë Baird's nomination as attorney general. It continued with the World Trade Center bombings and the Central Intelligence Agency shootings, both blamed on foreigners who had manipulated the immigration system. Chinese smuggling ships, Haitian boat people,

Cuban rafters, and all those who had slipped across the southern border seemingly at will created the cumulative impression of a nation incapable of exercising sovereignty over its borders. The political climax in this series of events came with the massive vote in favor of Proposition 187 in November 1994. American immigration policy, it seems safe to say, will never be the same.

California governor Pete Wilson, a Republican, said during the 1994 campaign, "Proposition 187, the 'Save Our State' initiative, is the two-by-four we need to make them take notice in Washington." Indeed, Wilson proved to be correct after Proposition 187 carried 59 percent of the vote in the nation's largest state. Throughout 1995, Washington produced dozens of plans to crack down on illegal immigration, reduce legal immigration, or limit immigrants' access to social welfare programs. Whether emanating from the Clinton administration, congressional committees, or the Commission on Immigration Reform led by the late Barbara Jordan, all these proposals sought to close America's doors to one degree or another. But as the 1996 election drew near, only the first steps had been taken toward any significant change in immigration policy.

Despite the political heat and rhetoric that it generates, immigration does not lend itself to quick fixes. And that is a good thing. The backlash against immigration epitomized by the Proposition 187 vote in 1994 has fundamentally changed the politics of immigration in America, calling attention to an immigration system that is woefully ineffective and that no longer enjoys the faith of the American people. A new approach is needed, but the laws, policies, and bureaucracies that govern immigration cannot and should not be created by sweeping omnibus reform measures. This has been the approach in the past, but it is inappropriate today.

The nation is currently in the midst of a mature migration that began three decades ago with changes in U.S. immigration laws, labor force demands, and foreign policies. By the 1990s, immigration was adding more than a million people a year to the U.S. population and, by 1994, 9 percent of the U.S. population was foreign-born—nearly double the percentage in 1970. Immigration to the United States now represents a huge and well-established demographic force with its own dynamic. The contemporary immigration flow involves millions of people in dozens of countries who have developed familial and economic connections to the United States—connections that have created the momentum for future influxes. Having encouraged the development of this human flow over the past thirty years, the United States will be hard-pressed to change its direction with a one-shot overhaul of immigration laws. Any attempt to manage such a powerful demographic force will require a consistent, long-term effort involving many steps and a great deal of flexibility.

To begin with, a new perspective is needed from which to debate immigration policies. Currently the issue is viewed as the challenge of enforcing sovereignty and controlling a flow of people that emanates from abroad. But the real challenge is to make immigration work to the nation's benefit, to understand how it relates to a variety of social and economic dynamics, to establish a set of goals and priorities, and then try to tailor the flow to these objectives. People can and will disagree over how much immigration is beneficial and how much is too much. My intent here is not to add to the copious but hollow debate over numbers. Instead, I hope to show that an extensive process of deliberation, study, and experimentation will be necessary before policymakers can reach any sensible decision over numbers. Moreover, that process of deliberation needs to be focused not on the borders or the population growth rates of third world countries but on America's cities and the needs of its economy.

Such a perspective necessarily demands a new policy framework. For most of this century immigration policy has been a congressional prerogative, shaped in a handful of big laws that took years to develop and that set down mandates intended to last for decades. A keen appreciation of how large-scale immigration is linked to a wide variety of domestic concerns requires a decision-making process that is more frequent and more responsive. Instead of setting immigration law in stone, Washington should be prepared to adjust its priorities regularly and shift resources in response to new needs at home and changes in the immigration flow from abroad. This more flexible policy framework would require a move toward something like a regulatory model of policymaking that involves the Congress and the executive branch more evenly. This would allow a long-term effort both to reduce the flow of illegal aliens and to exercise greater control over the dynamic process of legal immigration.

THE IMMIGRATION BACKLASH

To understand the immigration backlash that swept the nation so forcefully in the mid-1990s, it helps to return to the story of Barbara Coe. Her visit to a social services center in the once overwhelmingly white town of Santa Ana, California, and what happened afterward tells a great deal about the politics of immigration in America today.

"I tried to find someone to help me but there were three windows to serve Spanish-speaking people, two for Asians, and one for English-speakers—and it was closed." Coe was seeking public health benefits for an elderly friend but was turned down. "So I asked this woman, this counselor, 'You tell me what's going on out there, what is it?' When the counselor told me that lots of those people waiting were illegal aliens and they were getting benefits instead of citizens like my friend, I walked out of there outraged. I decided I had to do something."

Coe was almost certainly misinformed about what was taking place in that office. Illegal aliens simply are not and never have been eligible for most forms of public assistance, and, given their fear of the law, would not be likely to crowd into a social services center. This fact, however, has not stopped a great many people from believing sincerely that illegal aliens have produced an explosion in welfare spending.

What Coe did perceive is the breakneck pace of demographic change in Southern California. Once an overwhelmingly white, middle-class area, Orange County is now home to the largest Vietnamese population outside of Ho Chi Minh City. As former military allies, the Vietnamese arrived as refugees, making them specially privileged legal immigrants with full rights to many benefits and services. And, like the rest of the region, Orange County has experienced a large influx of Latinos that includes many legal immigrants eligible for public assistance. Along with them came illegals, who are not eligible.

When Coe left that government office building in 1992, she quickly discovered that many people across Southern California shared her outrage. Looking for quick results, Coe joined forces with a group of Orange County political activists who had hit upon the idea of using a ballot initiative to combat illegal immigration in the same way that angry, middle-class white voters had fought property taxes in 1978 by passing Proposition 13, which froze tax rates for existing homeowners.

Proposition 187 would prohibit illegal immigrants from receiving social or welfare services, ban them from public schools and universities, and prevent them from receiving publicly funded health care except in emergencies. Everyone seeking these benefits would have to document immigration or citizenship status, and administrators would be obliged to report "suspected" illegal immigrants to the authorities.

Along with many other election results in 1994, the overwhelming vote in favor of Proposition 187 reflected a widespread anxiety centered on, but not limited to, white middle-class voters. But it was a cry for help, not a workable plan of assistance. Weeks before the election it became clear that Proposition 187 would face paralyzing court tests because it raised so many constitutional questions and ran afoul of so many precedents. In fact, less than twenty-four hours after the polls closed, both federal and state judges issued restraining orders prohibiting implementation of the initiative, and there is every reason to assume that the legal challenges will stretch out for years to come.

None of that bothered Coe and her colleagues. They readily admit that their proposition was a distress call. The use of public services by illegal aliens may have been the literal focus of Proposition 187, but as a piece of political theater it carried a much broader message. Public opinion polls and other evidence pointed to concerns among Proposition 187 supporters about their economic well-being that went far beyond the issue of public services. These voters were not primarily the kind of low-wage workers likely to compete for jobs with immigrants, especially illegal immigrants. And it is simplistic to view the anti-immigration backlash as a racist response to an influx of Asians and Latinos. If this were true, one would expect to see other efforts to enforce racial separation or claim racial prerogatives, none of which have been forthcoming. Proposition 187 is most clearly read as part of an overall reaction to wide-ranging changes, of which immigration is among the most dramatic.

In California the impact of immigration has been magnified by several other factors. Strict limits on property tax rates and mismanagement by local officials have seriously degraded the quality of public services that were once the envy of the nation. Vast suburban tracts that had spoken of new horizons when first built in the 1960s and 1970s were beginning to seem crowded and worn out. A growing outmigration of whites to the Pacific Northwest and the Rocky Mountain states added to the doubts of those who stayed behind. And whatever illusions remained about Southern California as the land of endless summer had been dashed at the beginning of the 1990s when the regional economy lapsed into the deepest and most painful recession since the end of World War II. All these factors found expression in anxiety over immigration, which put a human face on an era of great change.

Since the mid-1960s, immigration has had an impact on every major urban area, but the intensity of the demographic change in Southern California is easy for outsiders to underestimate because no other part of the nation has experienced anything like it since the turn of the century. In the 1990 census the foreign born made up 37 percent of the population in the Los Angeles metropolitan area, and by the mid-1990s this figure probably matched or surpassed the 40 percent mark scored by New York in 1910 at the peak of the European migration.

It is a big change and it came quickly. The early twentieth century influx of immigrants from Southern and Eastern Europe ended when Congress passed the National Origins Act of 1924, which effectively excluded all newcomers except those from Northern Europe. The depression and World War II then shut off the flow across the Atlantic. No significant number of immigrants entered the country again until after 1965, when Congress enacted a major change in the law opening the doors to immigrants from Latin America and Asia. Economic changes in the United States created new appetites for immigrant workers in a variety of niches, from the low-wage service sector to the medical staffs of big city hospitals. And the cold war caused important new flows either as a result of Communist actions, such as those that spurred Cuban exiles or Soviet Jews, or as a by-product of U.S. initiatives, which contributed to the proliferation of Vietnamese boat people and Central American asylum seekers.

The result was a sudden demographic change. For half a century between the 1920s and 1970s, very few immigrants came to America. Then, when that pause ended, a rush began. Between 1975 and 1995, three million more people joined the population as legal immigrants than during the preceding fifty years. If one adds the commonly accepted estimates of illegal immigration, that figure roughly doubles to about six million more people than during the entire fifty-year pause. And more than a third of all the new immigrants live in California.

The anxiety that accompanies a huge demographic change of this sort inevitably generates blame. In California and much of the rest of the country the blame landed squarely on Washington. Almost every major call for greater immigration controls—whether from a tempered voice such as Barbara Jordan's or a shrill one such as Pat Buchanan's—included hefty criticism of the federal government for having failed in its responsibility to guard the borders and maintain an effective immigration system.

The 1994 elections produced a rush to make new immigration policies, just as they produced a rush to reform welfare and balance the federal budget. When policymakers turned their attention to all these issues, the overarching political goal was to defuse voter anger over sins of the past. Washington would do penance for letting a threatening phenomenon get too big, and this applied to the number of immigrants just as it did to the number of people on welfare and the number of dollars in the federal deficit. The one clear goal in each case was to get the numbers down. Beyond this, at least as far as immigration is concerned, not much forward thinking went into deciding what the future should look like. No consensus was developed around priorities and purposes for the immigration system except that it should let fewer foreigners live in the United States. Inevitably, this kind of policymaking produces only temporary solutions. A new direction may have been set, one that seeks to close America's doors, but the process of defining a new immigration policy had barely begun.

A NEW LANDSCAPE, A NEW DIRECTION

Shifts in immigration policy generally have followed shifts in the political landscape. Criticism of the racial and ethnic bias in the national origins system began to mount in the 1950s, reflecting new attitudes bred in the civil rights era. Legislation ending the national origins system was adopted in 1965 as part of the civil rights reforms that followed the huge Democratic victory in the 1964 elections. For much of the next three decades opponents of restriction could effectively combat proposals to reduce immigration by calling them "racist."

After 1965 virtually every new step in immigration policy produced an increased influx. It took almost constant debate from the early 1970s to 1986 for Washington to produce a law aimed at controlling illegal immigration, and the law was so thoroughly compromised by the time it was enacted that it had little permanent effect on the illegal flow. Then in 1990 Congress revised the legal immigration system in a way that boosted the number of permanent visas issued each year by roughly a third from about 600,000 to

800,000. An additional 300,000 to 400,000 illegal immigrants were added to the nation's population yearly according to widely accepted estimates by the Immigration and Naturalization Service (INS).

In the mid-1990s the drive to close the doors and end the current era of immigration reflected a fundamental shift in the direction of American politics, a shift that went far beyond immigration. The 1994 election illuminated a new political landscape marked by torrents of citizen anger. The Proposition 187 vote showed that immigrants, especially when present in large numbers, could provoke as much hostility in the electorate as federal bureaucrats, coddled criminals, or "welfare queens." Something had changed in the public psyche regarding immigration. National polls began to show that a great majority of people thought there was simply too much immigration, even if they did not identify individual immigrants with any particular problems.

For triumphant congressional Republicans, putting limits on immigration seemed to fit neatly with the "revolution" they had promised. When the new GOP-led Congress arrived in Washington in January 1995, wide-ranging immigration reform was added to an already ambitious agenda.

Within months, sweeping immigration bills were churning out of Congress, the Commission on Immigration Reform had offered its plan, and the Clinton administration had chimed in with some ideas of its own. Every one of these options represented a sharp departure from thirty years of welcoming immigration policies. Their clear intent was to decrease the number of immigrants, both legal and illegal, and decrease it sharply. However, lawmakers quickly came to realize that accomplishing that intent would not be quick or simple. Although the desire for an immigration overhaul was nearly unanimous, there was no consensus over specific measures. Many in the business community did not want to lose the freedom to import foreign workers. Some politicians in both parties opposed cuts in family immigration because they either sympathized with or feared the political wrath of growing Latino and Asian communities. Libertarians objected to the creation of a national workers' registry and other enforcement proposals they viewed as encroachments on individual freedoms.

It seemed that a preponderance of opinion favored a more restrictive system, at least for illegal immigration, but it remained to be seen how far the nation was prepared to go, who would be asked to make sacrifices, and what new standards would be developed for selecting new legal immigrants. Even if there had been agreement on the desired outcomes, these are issues that defy quick solutions.

Bringing the rate of immigration down is no simpler a task than bringing down federal spending. Deficit reduction became a national cause in the early 1980s. Despite worthy pronouncements, good intentions, and some sweeping legislation aimed at controlling the budget, deficit spending continued to grow throughout the decade. A full fifteen years later, after several budget crises and fiscal reforms, deficit control remains something the nation can only struggle toward. Expressions of political will do not make it any easier to assign sacrifices, and so, even after the federal shutdowns and the White House showdowns of 1996, it remains clear that real deficit reduction will still require years of determined action and tough choices.

So, too, will immigration control develop as a political priority over a long period of time and require repeated efforts by Washington policymakers. Like a balanced budget, an effective immigration policy cannot be decreed but must be elaborated, refined, and periodically revisited.

The most important assignment for the future will be to create an overall policy design that links immigration to a broad understanding of national goals. In response to the 1994 election, Congress and the Clinton administration set about making immigration laws, not policies. They did not attempt to determine how the flow of newcomers should fit into the nation's needs for labor, how it relates to America's demographic future, or how to weigh immigration's benefits and its costs. The answer to those kinds of questions will await the next round of policymaking, which is likely to follow the 1996 election.

THE CONCEPT OF LINKAGE

One year after California voters approved Proposition 187, Senator Alan K. Simpson (R-Wo.) rose on the Senate floor to argue that "curbing, even stopping, illegal immigration is not enough." With a speech in November 1995, he introduced a bill to make deep cuts in the number of legal immigrants allowed into the country, whether for employment, for family reunification, or as refugees.

Legal immigration at the levels experienced since the late 1980s constituted a clear danger to America's poor unskilled workers, to its college students, and to its most skilled technicians, he said. "For too many U.S. workers, the impact of immigration includes adverse effects on their own wages and individual job opportunities."

But the backlash was not just a matter of economics. Simpson said the public had become "increasingly restless and dissatisfied" with a growing immigrant influx that was transforming the very fabric of the nation, and that it would be satisfied only with a "fundamental change" in immigration policy. "The American people," Simpson said, "are so very fed up with being told—when they want immigration laws enacted which they believe will serve their national interest and when they also want the law to be enforced—that they are being cruel and mean-spirited and racist. They are fed up with efforts to make them feel that Americans do not have that most fundamental right of any people: to decide who will join them here and help form the future country in which they and their posterity will live."

The leading Republican voice on immigration policy since the early 1980s, Simpson was unapologetic about the breadth of his concerns or the dimensions of the cure he was prescribing. Immigration in all its forms had to be reduced drastically, Simpson concluded. "It is time to slow down, to reassess, to make certain we are assimilating well the extraordinary level of immigration the country has been experiencing in recent years."

Simpson and other advocates of restriction gave voice to widespread anxiety about the way immigration touched on other aspects of American life, from cultural identity to economic security. Many of those fears were based on exaggerated assumptions about immigration's negative impact, but at the same time they reflected accurate perceptions that the presence of immigrants was changing the country in important ways. For example, English faces no threat as the dominant language of the United States despite the concerns of those who have proposed laws to enshrine it as the nation's "official" language. But it is true that the influx of immigrant children needing to be taught English adds significantly to the problems of already overburdened urban school systems. The effects of immigration are not as bad as the hard-line restrictionists contend, nor are they as insignificant as proponents of open-door policies would argue.

It is essential to grasp the scope of immigration's impact if we are to understand the range of public policy options likely to be debated through the end of the decade. The public reaction has focused attention on the way immigration affects everything from welfare usage to job availability in high-tech industries. This has created the political context for a wide-ranging reassessment of immigration policies. For example, in 1995 Congress voted on various measures designed to stop legal immigrants from getting certain types of health and welfare benefits because of widespread, though inflated, reports that the United States was becoming a haven for elderly foreigners malevolently seeking easy retirement incomes. Immigration policy has developed with many different objectives in the past, but until recently attacking Medicaid fraud had never been one of them.

As the anti-immigrant backlash spread, the variety of problems attributed to immigrants multiplied. Regardless of the many misapprehensions involved, fear set the proper context for a new immigration debate. Even if many people exaggerated the damage done by immigration, it is appropriate to examine immigration from a broad perspective and to explore its implications for many different areas of public policy.

As the nation begins what is sure to be a long process of refining its immigration system, the goal of the debate should be to find linkages to the many other aspects of national policy affected by immigration. Effective immigration laws cannot be drafted in isolation from other concerns. For example, at the most basic level, immigration policy must be linked to manpower priorities. What kind of workers and how many of them does the economy need? How well can those needs be forecast, and how precisely can immigrant flows be managed to meet them? More difficult questions arise in terms of the nation's demographic priorities. How much or how little population growth does the nation want to derive from immigration? How far should the government go in determining the ethnic or racial content of that population growth?

In this regard, regulating immigration resembles the setting of tax policies. Government action in these areas can have a huge influence over the entire nation. New policies can be targeted to act as agents of change in specific areas of society. But neither tax nor immigration policies are an end in themselves; rather, they are means to an end. Taxes are raised to finance the actions of government. So, too, immigration should be envisioned as demographic fuel for economic and social growth.

Misunderstood Risks and Passive Policies

Throughout the early 1990s the nation's television screens were filled with images that reinforced fears that the United States was the helpless target of millions of unwanted migrants from all over the world. A nation that had been protected by two oceans from the worst ravages of war for so long suddenly saw itself as vulnerable to a different kind of invasion.

This previously unthinkable sense of geographic vulnerability may be one of the most subtle and potent sources of the anxiety caused by immigration. And the perceived threat was massive and widespread. The "entire Third World" became an important demographic concept as the immigration backlash developed. Some advocates of restrictive policies proclaimed the existence of a veritable subspecies of human beings with distinct characteristics: they lived primarily in warm climates, they were not white, they were poor and badly educated, they reproduced so quickly that they existed in infinite supply, and they all wanted to come to the United States.

The most extreme version of such views gained little currency mostly because of distaste for the radical policies they imply. However, a wide range of much more moderate options are informed by the same underlying assumption that the world is crowded with an undifferentiated mass of humanity looking enviously northwards. In presenting his proposals to reduce legal immigration Senator Simpson decried the "hundreds of millions" of people around the world who would like to come live in the United States.

This is the demographic premise—a massive collection of human beings waiting for the opportunity to come here—that fuels the fear of immigration. The Cuban rafters, Mexican border jumpers, and Chinese smugglers' ships are shocking enough in themselves, but they provoked such a deep reaction because they were perceived as the first waves of a much larger invasion.

Virtually all proposals for restriction are based on a simple construct: immigration pressures are generated in the world outside our borders, and immigration policies must serve as a barrier that withstands that pressure and controls access to the nation. This assumption is not advanced just by restrictionists. Until recently, it also informed a great deal of academic research and the advocacy of those who favor high levels of immigration.

Throughout the mid-1990s the debate has been between those who feel that current levels of immigration are good for the country or at worst do no harm and those who feel the numbers should come down. Either way the basic principle is the same: the human pressure is on the outside, and immigration policy is the control valve. In fact, this premise is incorrect and deceptive.

First, there is no undifferentiated demographic pressure that characterizes immigration. People come to the United States from relatively few specific places, not equally from the whole of the world. Each of these flows has developed out of its own history and has unique characteristics in terms of the kinds of people who come, where in the sending society they come from, and where they end up in the United States. Rather than a uniform pressure from outside, overall immigration is a collection of thousands of different individual flows. Rather than water pouring from a faucet depending on how far it is opened, immigration is like electricity coming through a bundle of multicolored wires each connecting with its own circuitry.

Second, the United States is not merely a passive receptor. It does not exercise an undifferentiated appeal for all persons living in less affluent nations. Instead, a variety of social and economic forces within the United States, such as job opportunities in a given sector of the economy, attract particular types of immigrants. The United States itself also creates circumstances that stimulate migrations. For example, the long-term presence of American military forces in the Philippines and Korea has helped generate a larger flow from those countries than from other Asian nations. And in some situations, U.S. government policies have been the most important stimulus of the influx. Mexican farmworkers, Hmong tribesmen from Laos, and Filipino nurses each represent flows instigated specifically by U.S. policies.

However, as the new debate over immigration developed in the mid-1990s most of the discussion continued to reflect these twin misapprehensions: that immigration is the result of a global demographic pressure and that the role of U.S. immigration policy is to act as a spigot regulating how much of that mass of humanity should be allowed to enter at a time.

These erroneous perceptions are deeply rooted in the history of U.S. immigration policies. Beginning with the Asian exclusion laws of the late nineteenth century, the United States attempted to control immigration with policies aimed at specific racial and ethnic groups. The intellectual basis for these policies was the thought that humanity could be divided into races and cultures with immutable characteristics and judged according to their desirability. (The domestic counterpart of this approach was Jim Crow segregation.) It produced widely accepted judgments that people of many nationalities were simply incapable of operating in a democracy and a free market economy. This trend in policymaking culminated with the National Origins Act of 1924 and its highly restrictive system of country-specific quotas.

When the Immigration Act of 1965 overturned that system, President Lyndon B. Johnson said, "Every American can be proud today because we have finally eliminated the cruel and unjust national origins system from the immigration policy of the United States. We have righted a long-standing wrong. So today, any man, anywhere in the world can hope to begin a new life of freedom and a new life of greater opportunity in the United States. No longer will his color or his religion or his nationality be a barrier to him."[2]

In 1924 the pendulum had swung toward the extreme of an immigration system based on specific racial, ethnic, and national preferences. Forty years later it swung back toward a system that viewed applicants from all over the world as members of a single pool of prospective immigrants. In rejecting the old system of preferences the nation also substantially rejected the broader idea of picking and choosing immigrants according to standards that judged their potential value to American society. Because the racist standards applied in the past had been so odious, the very idea of selecting immigrants to suit a national purpose was discredited.

Instead of national origins, family relations became the key criterion for gaining admission to the United States. A relatively small number of foreigners entered the country on special visas linked to their employment. Others arrived as refugees or asylum seekers, most of them fleeing Communist countries. But the vast majority of immigrants were judged only by their kinship to people already in the United States. Under the family preference system all siblings of U.S. citizens were treated equally, as were all adult children of legal permanent residents. It didn't matter where they came from, whether they were rich or poor, educated or illiterate.

The system of immigration policies that developed after 1965 has had a variety of consequences that will be examined in greater detail in later chapters, but it is important to note here that these policies developed out of a new perspective on immigration—a perspective that now shapes the way most Americans think about the issue.

By rejecting as racist the notion that immigrants of certain nationalities are undesirable, the United States adopted a perspective that viewed all prospective immigrants as equals. The new policy was born out of the logic of the civil rights movement and a moral imperative to avoid even the semblance of discrimination. Over the years, though, it has had a distorting impact on immigration, an area of policy that involves not the recognition of rights held by citizens but the granting of privileges to those petitioning for entry from abroad.

The perceptions that formed the basis for this policy and the policy itself encouraged the feeling that an undifferentiated mass of people lay beyond the borders eager to enter. Americans also came to feel that their immigration system was powerless to decide who among these people should be admitted. The system seemed to be based on a "first come, first served" approach, and in many respects that was the case.

Over time, the moral imperatives of the 1960s lost their salience in American society. This was no less true of the new direction set in immigration policies than for affirmative action or the welfare safety net. The political foundation for the reform policies of the civil rights era eroded, and the policies themselves became a source of resentment among many Americans who believed that they granted false entitlements.

Americans have lost faith in the immigration system. This in turn has fueled fear of immigrants and anger toward the federal government. It is unlikely that faith can be restored simply by trying to close the nation's doors. Instead, such an approach might heighten the feeling that the nation is under siege. What is required is an immigration system that begins by looking inward and assessing how immigration can be used to further the nation's goals.

TOWARD AN ACTIVIST APPROACH

Responding to the backlash, political leaders of both parties reflexively put forward proposals to shut the doors. These proposals were based on the same premises as the policies they were attempting to reverse. When America opened its doors between 1965 and 1990, it looked out to the world, saw a seemingly infinite supply of prospective immigrants, decided to treat them for the most part equally, and created an immigration policy that simply controlled the number of people allowed into the country. The world view of those who proposed closing the doors in the mid-1990s was only slightly different, although they saw prospective immigrants pushing for admission and getting in all too often, sometimes deviously.

Whether the goal was to be welcoming or restrictive, immigration policy has been considered a passive matter, a gate-keeping function. Most recently the temptation has been to see immigration policy defensively, as a negative choice about keeping people away.

By far the largest response to illegal immigration in recent years has been to rapidly expand the Border Patrol. While an effective border policy is better than the chaos of the past, a successful policy on illegal immigration also will involve making decisions about the future of the low-wage workforce, how the government should police workplaces, and how access to public services should be controlled.

Proposals to limit the flow of legal immigrants have involved mostly setting lower numbers for various visa categories. But over the long run, deciding the composition of legal immigration also will involve admission policies for the nation's colleges and graduate schools and the recruiting practices of top corporations as well as housewives in search of nannies.

Instead of beginning with the unhappy assumption that the United States needs to keep most of the world from crashing its party, this nation is in the enviable position of being able to choose which guests to invite to its banquet. These choices, however, must evolve from decisions about the nation's needs and goals. America can be an active conduit of the immigration flow rather than a passive receiver, but only if it knows what it wants out of the process. Creating such a framework for immigration policy will take time. And it will be a difficult task in a nation as profoundly uncertain about its identity and its future as the United States in the mid-1990s.

But immigration demands a response and, as such, it may become one of the means by which America is forced to resolve its uncertainties. Deciding new immigration policies based on an assessment of the nation's needs and goals should be seen as a great opportunity. Immigration debates historically have provoked an unusual degree of self-examination because high levels of immigration put the nation's very identity in play. More so than many other controversies, immigration obliges people to ask themselves what they want their nation to become.

CHAPTER 2

THE CHALLENGES OF A
MATURE MIGRATION

Any new framework for U.S. immigration policy must begin with an understanding of the dimensions and character of the current flow. The first of these factors is easy to assess: it is big and getting bigger. According to Census Bureau estimates, the foreign-born population of the United States reached 22.6 million people in 1994, accounting for 8.7 percent of the total population—the highest proportion since World War II and nearly double the percentage in 1970. Since the late 1980s, one million or more people a year have come to the United States with the intent of taking up residence here, legally or illegally.[3]

The second factor, the character of the flow, is paradoxical. It is both new and old. By all indications it is accelerating, yet it is also a mature demographic event that follows distinct, well-developed patterns. The current wave of immigration began to gain momentum in the mid-1970s, following a hiatus of nearly fifty years. At the turn of the century, the United States admitted between 600,000 and one million (or more) immigrants each year—levels not reached again until the 1980s. From the mid-1920s to the mid-1970s the average was about 250,000 a year. The United States is currently experiencing a new wave of immigration quite distinct from the European wave, but it is also an event that is now into its third decade.

The Census Bureau estimates that about one-fifth of the foreign-born population in 1994, some 4.5 million people, had entered the country since 1990, with another 8.3 million people having arrived in the 1980s. This means that the United States is absorbing a large number of people who have been here for a relatively short time (see Figure 2.1).

At the same time, this population comes from relatively few places around the world (see Table 2.1) and concentrates itself in only a few parts of the United States (see Figure 2.2). Mexico alone accounted for nearly 6.3 million people in the 1994 Census Bureau estimates. Mexican immigrants, together with those from just two Caribbean countries (Cuba and the Dominican Republic), make up more than a third of the total foreign-born population.

The smaller Asian influx includes substantial flows from two countries that have been traditional sources of immigrants (China and the Philippines), as well as from countries that have only recently become major senders (such as Korea, Vietnam, and India) and that have quickly established large communities in the United States.

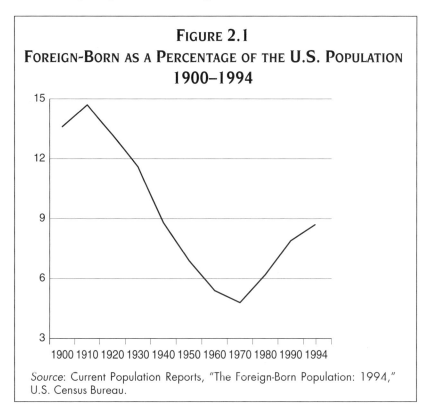

FIGURE 2.1

FOREIGN-BORN AS A PERCENTAGE OF THE U.S. POPULATION 1900–1994

Source: Current Population Reports, "The Foreign-Born Population: 1994," U.S. Census Bureau.

TABLE 2.1
TOP TEN COUNTRIES OF BIRTH FOR IMMIGRANTS ADMITTED IN 1994

Mexico	111,398
China (PRC)	53,985
Philippines	53,535
Dominican Republic	51,189
Vietnam	41,345
India	34,921
Poland	28,048
Ukraine	21,010
El Salvador	17,644
Ireland	17,256

Source: Immigration and Naturalization Service

FIGURE 2.2
FOREIGN-BORN POPULATION BY STATE OF RESIDENCE 1994

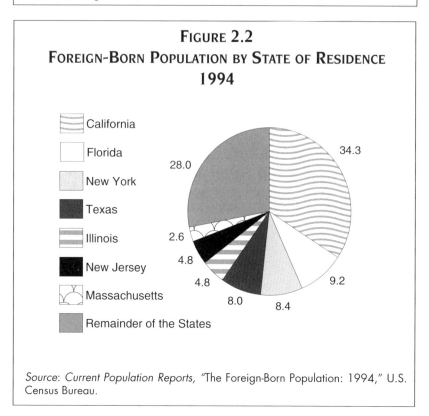

California
Florida
New York
Texas
Illinois
New Jersey
Massachusetts
Remainder of the States

34.3
28.0
9.2
8.4
8.0
4.8
4.8
2.6

Source: Current Population Reports, "The Foreign-Born Population: 1994," U.S. Census Bureau.

Meanwhile, about 60 percent of the total immigrant population has set up residence in just four states: California, Florida, New York, and Texas.

OLD CHANNELS, NEW NICHES, AND CONCENTRATION EFFECTS

These seemingly familiar facts mask huge policy challenges. The size of the flow ensures that the immigration issue will be a matter of concern for years, probably for decades, to come. Immigrants and their children now account for half of the nation's population growth. Something so big doesn't go away quickly.

Similarly, a long-term effort is suggested by the fact that so much of contemporary migration to the United States has deep roots. The Mexican influx has ebbed and flowed since the turn of century, meaning that there are communities in the United States linked to communities in Mexico by three generations of immigration. Many other countries, such as Cuba, the Dominican Republic, and the Philippines, have immigration channels that date back to the 1960s.

These flows have become part of the fabric of life in both the sending countries and in the United States. They constitute patterns of human behavior at both ends of the immigrant's voyage that are not easily altered or interrupted. For example, the 1991–92 recession was powerful enough to cause considerable disruption in the United States, including sufficient anxiety among American voters to help derail the reelection campaign of an otherwise popular president, George Bush. Even during this downturn, however, the number of legal immigrants continued to grow and to grow quickly. Such old and durable immigrant flows are not likely to respond readily to strokes of the pen in Washington.

In addition to established channels of immigration, new immigrant flows can arise rapidly, often in response to the availability of new niches in the U.S. economy. For example, India, which produced fewer than 2,000 immigrants in the 1950s, sent more than 250,000 in the 1980s, many of whom rapidly established a major presence in several fields of work, ranging from motel ownership and management to computer programming. Between 1980 and 1990, the number of countries with at least 100,000 immigrants living in the United States almost doubled.

Finally, the fact that the immigrant population is intensely concentrated in a few areas of the country means that this issue is subject to considerable distortion both as a political and a practical matter.

Some 34 percent of the total foreign-born population lives in California—a concentration nearly four times greater than any other state, including the runner-up, Florida. This means that California, especially Southern California, has become an anomaly and is treated as such by policymakers. Like New York in the first half of this century, Southern California differs markedly in its basic character from any other place in the country because it hosts so many immigrants. This poses immediate and vexing challenges that will color the development of immigration policy in the short term. The first of these is: Who pays?

The costs of immigration are paid primarily at the local level. These include the added burdens on education and health systems, the administrative difficulties of dealing with a population of non-English speakers, and the economic dislocations that can be caused by a steady influx of new immigrant workers. Some of the benefits of immigration, such as the revival of deteriorating residential neighborhoods and the growth of small business, are enjoyed locally, but for the most part the benefits of immigration are derived primarily at the national level. These include a more mobile and flexible labor force, the constant augmentation of the talent pool with adults who were educated and trained elsewhere (and at someone else's expense), and the ability to use immigration as a foreign policy tool.

This imbalance between local costs and national benefits becomes especially acute when newly arrived immigrants cluster in a few places while they go through the most costly period of adaptation to American society, then move into other parts of the country either later in life (or when the second generation moves out) when their contributions are greater. This happened in the era of European immigration, and it appears to be happening again now.

A second challenge is to develop a national political consensus about immigration policy. As a political matter, past immigration has had no real national constituency for or against it. In general, it has been treated by Congress as a bipartisan issue, and it has never (in living memory) been a major issue in a presidential campaign.

This is changing, however, in large part because the immigrant population is now concentrated in a few big states that exercise enormous influence in presidential elections. (Under the rules of the electoral college system, it takes 270 electoral votes to become president. These votes are decided by state on a winner-take-all basis. California alone has 54 votes, making it the keystone for almost any electoral strategy. In a close race, a few hundred thousand votes in Southern California can tip the state and contribute to a presidential victory.)

A presidential candidate cannot afford to ignore immigration even if only a relatively small number of strategically located voters feel passionately about it. California's political veto power is magnified by the fact that thus far no substantial popular constituency has emerged to defend open immigration policies. Moreover, for a great many Americans, immigration slips readily into a broader litany of discontent with federal policies, and those who feel this way have been willing to go along with proponents of greater restrictions.

Immigration is an area of policy that cries out for national consensus. Indeed, no broad direction can be set for immigration policy without some agreement on the national goals it seeks to accomplish. However, the high concentration of immigrants in just a few places creates distortions that make this kind of broad perspective much more difficult to reach.

THE HOURGLASS EFFECT

Immigration politics and policy are further complicated by wide disparities in the economic and educational status of immigrants. The immigrant population includes both rich and poor, educated and illiterate. Compared to the average American, some immigrants are better off while others are worse off. As such, immigrants elicit both envy and disdain.

The remarkable polarization evident in the foreign-born population comes through most clearly in their levels of education upon arrival, as surveyed by the Census Bureau in 1994. (See Table 2.2.)

Recent adult immigrants—those who arrived since 1990 and are at least twenty-five years old—are more likely to have a college degree than native-born Americans by a large margin (21 percent, as compared to 15 percent). The gap is even wider as one moves higher up the educational ladder. While 11.5 percent of recent immigrants have graduate and professional degrees, only about 7.5 percent of native-born Americans have achieved that level of schooling. At the same time, a full 36 percent of the adult immigrant population has not graduated from high school, compared with only 17 percent of the native population.

TABLE 2.2
EDUCATIONAL ATTAINMENT OF THE FOREIGN-BORN POPULATION—1994

	Native	Total	Foreign-Born Entry before 1980	Entry after 1980
Total 25 years and older	147,067	16,445	9,133	8,310
Not H.S. grad	25,166	6,274	3,164	3,109
H.S. grad/some college	89,382	7,147	4,069	3,076
Bachelor's degree	21,660	2,596	1,208	1,388
Grad. or prof. degree	10,859	1,428	692	737

Source: Current Population Reports, "The Foreign-Born Population: 1994," U.S. Census Bureau.

Immigrants' skills are mirrored in their incomes. About 10 percent of all immigrant workers who arrived after 1980 earned $35,000 a year or more, according to the 1994 Census survey. Even though the comparable figure for native-born Americans is 19 percent, immigrants' achievements at the high end are remarkable, given that most of them have been in the country for less than a decade and are still going through that period of adjustment when immigrant incomes are traditionally lowest. At the other end of the spectrum, more than 46 percent of the foreign-born workers who arrived since 1980 earned less than $10,000, while fewer than 35 percent of the native-born had incomes at that low a level.

Commenting on these characteristics, Philip L. Martin, an economist at the University of California, Davis, writes,

These immigrants differ from natives in education, income, and prospects for success. The United States and most other industrial countries have fostered diamond-shaped income distributions, with most of the population in the middle classes. The income distribution for immigrants by contrast, has an hourglass shape, since they tend to be

bunched at the extremes of the education and income
spectrum; many are college-educated professionals, and
even more are unskilled workers without high school
educations.[4]

While the foreign born do not mirror the U.S. population, neither do they reflect the world beyond America's borders. If immigrants were representative of the nations that sent them their
qualifications would be even more heavily weighted toward the
low end of the training scale. The United States is not simply repli-
cating itself with foreign-born workers, nor is it being colonized by
the Third World. Instead, immigration reflects the American future.

The educational characteristics of the foreign born are in
demand in the newest and fastest-growing segments of the
American labor market, such as high-tech manufacturing, finance,
and services, all of which require workers with either exceptional
training or little at all. America's rapidly evolving, postindustrial
economy offers diminished opportunities and rewards for those in
the middle, and it is in this vast center of the workforce where the
greatest numbers of native-born workers compete for available
jobs. Meanwhile, immigrants at either extreme find new jobs opening up for them.

Immigration has often satisfied the emerging demands of a
changing economy. At the turn of the century, the European influx
fed America's conversion to an urbanized and industrialized nation.
But, especially at the beginning of that process—when America's
character was still defined by small towns and rural life—few pre-
dicted that a blue-collar workforce made up of immigrants and
their children would become a great engine of American strength
and stability.

Now, as that industrial workforce and the economy it built
fade from the scene, a new economy and a new workforce is
emerging, and immigration is again contributing to the process.
For policymakers this means that immigration becomes a part of
the unpredictability and controversy that accompanies any broad
process of economic and social change.

To the extent that immigration is a source of workers for new
and growing sectors of the economy, it becomes difficult to forecast the
long-term economic effects of the influx. Also, the industries in which
immigrants work may lack a political constituency because they do not
meet well-known and easily defensible national economic needs.

When immigrants play a secondary role in a process of change, their contributions are not immediately obvious. For example, foreign-born doctors have become the primary workforce in urban public hospitals to such an extent that it appears to many causal observers that they have usurped a whole category of jobs previously held by natives. In fact, immigrants have moved into these jobs at a time when medicine has become not only an expanding profession for the native born but also one that is increasingly suburbanized and specialized. Indeed, immigrant doctors often fill vital but unrewarding jobs that do not attract native-born doctors.

Even in industries that traditionally have employed immigrants, such as apparel manufacturing, foreign-born workers have been part of a process of transformation. While much of the garment industry has moved to cheaper labor markets overseas, some areas of the business, such as women's sportswear, have remained in the United States and become dependent on immigrant labor. A pliant, low-wage workforce made up overwhelmingly of immigrants has allowed the development of a new industry that stresses speed, flexibility, and quality control in order to compete with manufacturers abroad.

The connection with economic change is not always clear when immigrants begin filling a niche in the labor force, so it is difficult to predict the practical results of changes in immigration policy. But the challenges posed by the character of the immigrant flow go far beyond mere unpredictability.

As Martin writes, "The hourglass shape of immigrant education and skills means that immigration reinforces the other factors that are promoting economic inequality by adding workers at the top and bottom of the labor force."

The native-born population has not been polarized yet into as much of an hourglass shape as the immigrant population, but it has been heading in that direction for several decades, with a smaller share of Americans gathering an ever-larger proportion of the nation's wealth at the top end, while the middle stagnates and the low-wage workforce grows.

Immigration may or may not accelerate the overall movement toward an hourglass society. Cause and effect are difficult to isolate when such huge and complex developments are under way. However, there is little doubt that immigrants "reinforce" this shift, as Martin says, and that they can readily be targeted as popular scapegoats for growing inequality. The foreign born who come here with education and skills and who succeed become representatives of a highly educated, highly entrepreneurial upper class that is far removed from the mainstream. The low-skill, low-income immigrants become representatives of an ever-larger, permanent underclass that seems alien and threatening.

Both as a practical and as a political matter the paradoxical character of contemporary immigration greatly complicates policymaking in this area. It is difficult to understand the economic roles played by the foreign born and assign them concrete values. In the meantime, immigrants acquire a range of symbolic values, most of them negative, as Americans grapple with an era of economic change.

A MATURE MIGRATION

Since the early days of this century, U.S. immigration law has included one provision or another designed to bar foreigners who are likely to become dependent on tax-supported social services. Although it may be the single most enduring element of immigration policy, the goal of preventing poor immigrants from becoming a drain on public resources received especially close attention in the mid-1990s.

Proposition 187 aimed at preventing illegal immigrants from receiving virtually any public service or benefit—not just welfare programs from which they are already barred but also medical care and education. Saving public funds was only one goal of this provision. The California initiative was meant to drive illegal aliens out of the state by creating an inhospitable, even unhealthy climate for them. Indeed, one of the reasons that the federal courts blocked implementation of the initiative was that it tried to usurp federal authority to set immigration policy.

Shortly after the passage of Proposition 187, an even more ambitious effort arose in Washington to limit access to services for legal immigrants. Even though Republicans and Democrats on Capitol Hill fought over almost every detail of welfare reform in 1995, they agreed from the start that one way to save money was to put new restrictions on the government help offered to immigrants when they fell on hard times. Provisions to keep immigrants from qualifying for a variety of means-tested welfare programs won ready agreement. But some provisions also blocked immigrants from receiving scholarship loans and grants. In several areas, immigrants would be prohibited from receiving public funds even after they became U.S. citizens. Although President Clinton vetoed the welfare reform bill in January 1996 and said it went too far in this area, he did not state any categorical opposition to reducing benefits to legal immigrants. Similar cuts were included in the welfare overhaul adopted by Congress in summer 1996 because they are among the few expedient means of reducing social spending.

The current emphasis on immigrant use of public services and benefits reflects a broader anxiety about the unharnessed growth of entitlement programs and concerns about the large number of immigrants who come to the United States poor and stay poor. But it also reflects an evolution in the immigrant population itself.

Young adults generally make up a disproportionately large part of an immigrant flow. This has been true across the ages because they are the travelers and adventurers in any society. Young adults tend to migrate alone rather than in family units, and single males often make up a large share of an immigrant population, especially in the early stages of a migration. For example, the 1994 Census survey found that nearly half of the foreign born who had entered the country since 1990 were between the ages of eighteen and thirty-four, compared with about a quarter of the general population in the same age range. Among the immigrants who came in the 1980s, men outnumbered women by 11 percent, although by the 1990s the gender ratio had nearly evened out.

Young adults do not tend to remain alone under any circumstances, and the difficulties of immigration encourage the formation of strong household structures and extended families. The immigrant flow may begin with single young people, but it does not remain that way.

Describing the European immigrants of the late nineteenth century, the historian John Bodnar writes, "Most immigrants, moreover, regardless of their class standing in the Old World or regional background were relatively young. They were at an age when they were more inclined to think about forming households of their own or sustaining one which had recently been initiated. Such a bunching of ages in the period of family formation could not but help the overall thrust toward familial and household organization."[5]

Single young adults are workers. They generally contribute to society and do not ask for much back. Families, on the other hand, usually have children who contribute nothing materially but require a great deal in the way of health and education. And once families are established, they often include the elderly of the previous generation, who also present substantial costs for needed care.

A mature migration involves very different policy challenges from an immigrant flow so fresh that it is characterized mainly by low-cost young adults. The current wave of immigration continues to bring a large proportion of people who are in the most productive phase of their lives, but the foreign-born population has been building for thirty years, and with considerable intensity for fifteen years. There is now a sizable group of people who have been in the United States long enough to form families and reach the point where their costs to society are on the rise. This has put immigrants' use of social benefits on the table as a major policy issue.

In this age of backlash the policy response has been to erect new barriers in the form of eligibility requirements that would limit drastically the number of immigrants who can gain access to public services and tax-supported benefits.

These new barriers are part and parcel of the much broader effort to reform a system of benefits originally intended to be a safety net for hard times, but now criticized as a vehicle for dependency on public largesse. As they apply to immigrants, these reforms are likely to produce a series of unintended consequences. Although the number of immigrants eligible for and making use of social benefits is on the rise, they do not belong to the target population at which the reforms aim. The foreign born are generally too new to America and to its welfare system to manifest the long-term problems, such as prolonged welfare use and disassociation from the labor market, that the reforms set out to resolve. Immigrants for the most part do not partake of the culture of dependency that is supposed to be combated through welfare-to-work plans and time limits on eligibility.

On the other hand, immigrants and their children do represent the fastest-growing source of workers for that sector of the economy marked by low wages, temporary employment, and thin profit margins. Therefore, in a prolonged economic downturn these legal immigrants would be prime candidates for the classic model of temporary, safety net social benefits that the reformers are most anxious to restore. Under the sweeping welfare reform plan passed in 1995 by both houses of Congress and vetoed by Clinton, legal immigrants would be turned away under such circumstances, regardless of whether they previously had been fully employed and self-sufficient, and in some cases regardless of whether they were American citizens.

A mature migration presents challenges beyond the realm of social benefits and the manner in which newcomers become integrated into American society. The initial step of simply determining how many immigrants to let into the country is different when a government is handling a wave of migration that has been under way for several decades, as opposed to one that is just beginning. At the start, the host nation can look at the whole world, as America did in the 1960s, set broad limits, and wait to see who shows up. Three decades later, the gatekeepers must deal with a migration that has developed a momentum and a direction of its own.

Managing a legal immigration policy based on family reunification is a far different matter when hundreds of thousands of families are divided between the United States and the sending countries than at the point when people are just beginning to move. Similarly, it is much more difficult to set visa limits after labor markets in the United States have become accustomed to receiving a steady stream of new workers from specific sending communities.

This points to an underlying factor that greatly complicates the decisionmaking process of the mid-1990s: to a large extent, the momentum and direction of the current influx were set by policy choices made in the past, and any new initiative must deal with the consequences of its predecessors. Setting new limits on immigration is not like setting a new national speed limit or a new set of minimum sentencing requirements for felonies. It is not simply a matter of picking a number and obliging everyone to live by it. Instead, it is more like setting interest rates or deciding emissions standards for industrial plants. Policymakers must deal with the expectations created by past decisions, as much as with the consequences of new ones. Congress wrestled with this in 1995 and 1996 as committees in both houses drafted bills reducing legal immigration and found themselves struggling to deal with a backlog of several million people who had applied for family reunification visas and remain on waiting lists. The challenge was not only to determine what was right for the future but also to do right by those who had made important decisions and investments based on existing policies.

A mature, well-developed migration of the sort that the United States is experiencing today does not lend itself to stroke-of-the-pen decisionmaking. It is impossible to start from scratch when confronting a demographic event that is three decades old and that involves nearly 20 million people in the United States and many millions more around the world. Rather than drastic or rapid changes, this is an area that demands decisions built upon past policies whenever possible. When departures from the past are essential, and sometimes they are, incremental moves are more likely to succeed than omnibus plans. It is always politically tempting to declare a crisis and promote a sweeping solution. But immigration usually defeats such gambits, and as it gains momentum and matures it becomes even more resistant to one-shot solutions.

CHAPTER 3

ILLEGAL IMMIGRATION:
A LEGACY OF AMBIVALENCE

On January 9, 1975, Immigration and Naturalization Service (INS) officials set up an early morning ambush at Battery Park on the southern tip of Manhattan. At 7:30 A.M. a ferryboat chugged up to the pier delivering a crew of laborers who had worked overnight doing maintenance on the Statue of Liberty. The INS officers sprang their trap and arrested two brothers who had been painting the statue. They were illegal aliens.

At the time, this was just the sort of incident to capture public attention. America's military prowess had been humbled in Vietnam at the hands of slightly built soldiers in black pajamas. Desert sheikhs had dealt a blow to America's economic sovereignty with the Arab oil embargo of 1973. A president had just self-destructed, and the economy was in deep recession. Americans could put up with a lot, but it was too much to contemplate foreigners sneaking into the country and taking jobs that rightfully belonged to U.S. workers.

Headlines such as "Illegal Aliens Painting Miss Liberty" became another emblem of American decline. Media reports trumpeted a seemingly unstoppable cascade of people across the Mexican border and told of shadowy figures taking jobs from worthy Americans. Immigration Commissioner Leonard F. Chapman,

Jr., a retired Marine Corps general, traveled the country promising that he could open up a million jobs for American workers "virtually overnight" if Congress would just give him enough men and money to seal the border and carry out mass deportations. Meanwhile, U.S. Representative Peter W. Rodino, Jr., the New Jersey Democrat who had gained a national voice as chairman of the Nixon impeachment hearings, was promoting legislation to outlaw the employment of illegals.[6]

In the dark days of the mid-1970s, illegal immigration became a hot second-tier issue. It may not have been as important as inflation, but it seemed easier to solve. This view turned out to be wrong. Inflation went away, but illegal immigration did not. Inflation came to be recognized as a profound structural problem that could be resolved only through a period of economic sacrifice and reordered expectations. Illegal immigration has persisted because policymakers refuse to recognize it as a structural issue as well, interwoven with basic economic trends, and insist on framing painless solutions. Illegal immigration never was and is not now nearly as big or as threatening a problem as inflation, so it is all the more surprising that it has proved so resistant to government control.

For the twenty years since illegal immigration first became a significant issue on the national agenda, it has prompted policies marked by a profound ambivalence in both their structure and their tone. Despite constant demagoguery about the dangers of illegal immigration, every proposal to control it has been so thoroughly compromised as to be rendered ineffective. This ambivalence persisted as the same range of options was debated time and again for two decades.

The lack of decisiveness has had several consequences. First, illegal immigration has increased and become a deeply entrenched phenomenon in both the United States and the sending nations. Second, anxiety over illegal immigration has deepened and spread to taint all immigration, legal or not. Finally, lost opportunities may be the worst legacy of ambivalent policymaking. In the mid-1980s, grand designs were put on the table, but they were implemented only as half measures. As a result they lost their effectiveness. Not only was that opportunity lost, but other options were also foreclosed. A decade later, in the mid-1990s, policymakers had little choice but to look for other, mostly harsher, possibilities.

A DIFFERENT KIND OF LAW ENFORCEMENT

The first attorney general forced to deal with demands for a crack-down on illegal immigration was Edward H. Levi of the Ford administration. He seemed reluctant to jump on the bandwagon, even reversing a Justice Department recommendation to issue a special document that all legitimate workers would have to show when applying for a job as a way of keeping illegals from entering the labor force.

Some people close to Levi said years later that, as a Jew, he felt particularly troubled by the prospect of identity cards, roundups, and deportations. And so, to defuse the mounting political pressure without taking drastic measures, Levi convened a cabinet com-mittee in 1975 to examine the problem of illegal immigration. To serve as executive director of the committee Levi reached down to one of the most junior officials in his department, Doris Meissner, who had been working for the government for less than two years and who had no experience with immigration policy.

Levi, a once and future University of Chicago law professor, summoned Meissner into the attorney general's conference room to give her the assignment. As Meissner recalls,

> I knew next to nothing about the subject and I listened attentively to get a fix on his ideas. I can remember him saying to me, "I don't know quite how we should handle this issue." He talked about how this was an area of law enforcement and that we needed effective laws. But he said this was different. It has to do with our identity and our traditions as a nation. It is a matter of who we want to be. The standards may have to be different. It may not be possible to get the same levels of compliance as in other areas of law enforcement or to use the same tactics.[7]

That philosophy became the foundation for U.S. policy toward illegal immigration for the next twenty years. The intentions may have been humanitarian, but so many people proved eager to exploit the cheap labor of illegal aliens that Levi's instructions pro-duced a policy framework built on trade-offs. It closed doors and opened them at the same time. It was illegal for these immigrants to be here, but no one made them leave. Until 1986, whenever an ille-gal alien got a job, the alien violated the law but the employer did not. After Congress outlawed the employment of illegals in 1986, it went an entire decade pointedly failing to give the government funding to enforce the law at even a symbolic level. Bizarre coalitions of Latino activists, civil libertarians, and a few niches of the business community like the California fruit and vegetable growers teamed up to defeat hardheaded initiatives. Levi's original goal was balance, but in the hands of special interests the result was equivocal. Some eighteen years later, in November 1993, when Doris Meissner returned to the same conference room to be sworn in as immigration commissioner, the same jury-rigged framework was still in place.

For two decades illegal immigration has been a topic of almost constant consternation in Washington. No one ever seriously disputed the fact that illegal immigration is not good for the country and often not good for the immigrants themselves. Recently, however, the evidence of the damage done by illegal immigration has mounted and gained credibility. A steady supply of workers with no recourse to the law has fueled a sector of the economy that survives beyond the bounds of government regulation. Though this may involve only a small portion of the workforce, perhaps 1 to 2 percent, numerous studies show that this shadow economy worsens wages and conditions for those least able to afford it. For some Latinos and Asians the persistence of large illegal populations has slowed the process of community building and has fostered the development of criminal organizations engaged in alien smuggling.

Immigration held a prominent place on the congressional agenda in the late 1970s and all through the 1980s, and then again in 1995. At least three administrations (Ford, Reagan, and Clinton) set up high-level interagency committees to look at the problem, and Congress twice created independent commissions that each spent years looking for solutions.

The same well-worn ideas—and often the same people—were brought forth to address the issue, with two main results: First, the illegal population of the United States grew larger, more permanent, and more accepted as it penetrated an ever-greater number of job categories, including some of the most personal, like child rearing. And, second, contrary to Levi's intent, the rhetoric and emotions of law enforcement eventually pervaded discussions of how America should admit and absorb newcomers from abroad. In the process, all immigrants—illegal, legal, even refugees from totalitarian regimes—came to be viewed with suspicion.

These two outcomes might seem contradictory. On the one hand, new immigrants, including illegal aliens, have become well-utilized, seemingly permanent fixtures in the American economy. On the other hand, they provoke hostility and the demand for crackdowns. In fact, a pained schizophrenia is the single, overarching result of the way immigration policy has developed over the past twenty years.

Illegal aliens violate the law by their very presence here, but, as Justice William J. Brennan, Jr., wrote in a 1982 U.S. Supreme Court decision guaranteeing the children of illegal aliens access to public education, they live in the United States "enjoying an inchoate federal permission to remain."[8]

This fundamental ambivalence—a class of people who are termed "illegal" by their very presence but who are not obliged to leave—has developed into a detailed policy structured on that ambivalence. The absence of effective policies in the 1970s and 1980s allowed the immigrant flow to develop momentum irrespective of U.S. national interests. And the failure to define clear goals meant that this huge demographic event occurred without any broad public understanding of its purpose. The specific policy compromises enacted in the past are important to understand because they now crop up at every turn and greatly complicate any effort to move in new directions.

BARGAINING AWAY A GREAT OPPORTUNITY

The chief outgrowth of the illegal immigration crisis of the mid-1970s was the creation of a congressional commission headed by the Reverend Theodore Hesburgh, president of the University of Notre Dame, which was charged with examining the whole of immigration policy. In 1981 the Hesburgh Commission produced a final report based on an idea so simple that it enjoyed a remarkable shelf life. The commission suggested that America should "close the back door" of illegal immigration so that it could "open the front door" of legal immigration. This principle remained the foundation of U.S. immigration policy into the 1990s.

Under the Hesburgh formulation it was politically safe to support tough action against illegal immigration even for advocates of open-door policies. After all, no one contended that illegal immigration was a good thing. If the strategies to end it were humanitarian and respected civil liberties, as the commission recommended, it would be hard to label the effort authoritarian or nativist, especially since the ultimate goal was to reinforce legal immigration. Ideally, the back door/front door plan should have laid the basis for decisive action against illegal immigration and for fortifying legal immigration. But things did not work out that way.

In deciding how to "close the back door," the Hesburgh Commission embraced an analysis that had been conventional wisdom since the mid-1970s: Illegal aliens come to the United States for jobs. Keep them from getting work and they won't come. As simple as the idea might seem, it suggested a major change in policy because, at the time, there was no penalty in federal law for an employer who hired illegal aliens. Throughout the 1970s and most of the 1980s, the INS would conduct raids on factories and farms, round up the illegals, and ship them home, but employers remained free to hire a new batch of illegals right away. The commission, along with advocates on both sides of the issue, considered this system ineffective and unjust.

Three Congresses considered the commission's recommendations to go after the "jobs magnet" before the Immigration Reform and Control Act won passage in 1986. That law for the first time imposed legal sanctions on the employers of illegal aliens. It became illegal to hire such a worker, and employers who did so would be subject to fines and other penalties depending on the severity of their offenses. That much of the law seemed simple and decisive, but no policies are simple or decisive when they are built upon a framework of ambivalence.

Employer sanctions were paired with a countervailing initiative: an amnesty for the existing illegal population. Like employer sanctions, the amnesty appealed to a wide swath of the interested parties. Advocates on all sides agreed that maintaining a large, permanent illegal population was not a healthy thing for the United States. Illegal immigrants, living in the shadows with no ready recourse to law enforcement, were easy targets for abuse by unscrupulous employers, landlords, and others. Their exploitation was not only an evil in itself but potentially lowered living standards for the people around them. No responsible policymaker suggested that illegal aliens should be rounded up and deported as they were in the 1950s. Instead, a broad consensus developed around the idea of an amnesty, provided it was accompanied by employer sanctions.

The goal was to address the entire problem at once. The sanctions would erase the motive for future illegal immigration. The amnesty would erase the legacy of the past. Put the two together and the nation could start with a clean slate. In retrospect it seems a noble design. It might have worked if there had been a complete amnesty that covered the entire illegal population and an enforceable sanctions law that really ended the employment of illegal aliens. But the effort to combat illegal immigration, built upon a foundation of ambivalence, evolved into a sequence of compromises and produced a law of half measures. As a result, the nation lost its last, best opportunity to solve the problem of illegal immigration with one bold stroke.

The movement from the clarity of the law's intention to the ambiguity of its implementation was most evident in the evolution of the amnesty program. The basic idea was to allow illegal aliens living in the country as of a given date to acquire the status of legal immigrants, but the terms of the amnesty, especially the cutoff date, provoked a fierce debate. Those most determined to end the illegals' underground existence—Latino groups, liberals, the Roman Catholic Church, some Jewish groups, and some labor unions—pressed for a date as close as possible to the time of enactment or implementation so that the amnesty would be as encompassing as possible. Other labor groups, many conservatives, and other restrictionists argued to push the date back into the past so that the amnesty would only cover illegals of long tenure in the country and so that the amnesty itself would not become a magnet, attracting illegals who would rush to the United States in the hopes of qualifying.

Congress eventually opened the amnesty to illegal aliens who had been living in the United States since 1982. Putting the date back several years was supposed to ensure that the amnesty applied only to people who had been continuous, long-term residents. As soon as that compromise had been achieved, however, California legislators, led by then Senator Pete Wilson, complained that the amnesty would not cover migrant farm workers who sometimes went back and forth across the border every year. The Californians in Congress insisted that their fruit and vegetable growers would lose their workforce unless special provisions were enacted to protect them. At first a guest-worker program was proposed, but the final settlement called for a separate, special amnesty that offered legal status to people claiming to have done seasonal agricultural work in the past.

Once the amnesties went into effect, nothing turned out as expected. The government had estimated that at least 2 million people would turn up for the regular amnesty. About 1.3 million actually did. The agricultural program was supposed to produce about 400,000 applicants. Nearly 1.8 million applied amid well-documented charges of massive fraud both by aliens and by many on the U.S. side, including some growers.

Over time, the amnesties proved to be the worst of both worlds. The nearly 3 million people who went into the program produced a giant logjam in the immigration system as they gained legal status and thus the right to sponsor relatives hoping to join them. (A decade after the law was enacted the logjam has yet to clear.)

Worse still, the program failed to produce the clean slate that its framers had originally envisioned. The amnesty recipients represented only about 60 percent of the illegal population at the time, according to INS estimates. Many had arrived after the 1982 cutoff date because the mid-1980s were some of the worst years of the Mexican economic crisis and the Central American civil wars. Others could not produce the necessary documentation proving they had lived in the United States continuously since 1982. And some Latino activists argued that not enough time and effort was expended by Washington to make sure that people came forward. Whatever the cause, a substantial portion of the illegal population remained illegal. It also meant that America's big cities continued to play host to the social networks and economic structures that facilitated illegal immigration in the first place, so the illegal population could grow again at will. The original goal of the amnesty program—to allow the country to start again with a clean slate—was critically compromised by the legislative bargains necessary to get it enacted.

Not only did the amnesties leave intact a large illegal population, but they also laid the groundwork for continued flows. Millions of households were created in which at least one person could rent housing, buy a car, and get a job legally, thus providing a safe haven for others who came illegally. Moreover, since a majority of the amnesty applicants, especially among Mexicans, were lone males, a new kind of illegal traffic developed for purposes of family reunification, as men now secure in their position here sent home for wives and children. Washington, deciding it could not break up these families, allowed the illegal relatives of amnesty recipients to remain and eventually apply for legal status themselves. At the end of 1995, some 824,000 such relatives still awaited visas. This backlog became a major obstacle when Congress set about trying to reform the legal immigration system in 1995–96.

The other half of the grand design—employer sanctions—was also compromised to the point that it, too, did not perform as intended. For more than a decade before employer sanctions finally were enacted as part of the 1986 law, there had been an almost continuous debate as to how they would be implemented. A key concern all along was that employers would bear the burden of determining whether a new hire was eligible to work or not and would face penalties if they made a mistake. Several ideas were put forth as a means of easing that burden. One of the most persistent of these involved the creation of some kind of system that would allow employers to verify easily the identity and work eligibility of a job applicant.

The proposals for such a system ranged from a national identity card to a computer registry based on Social Security numbers. Regardless of the technical means involved, each proposal would require the participation to some degree or another of every employer and every member of the workforce, including every native-born American holding a job or likely to seek one. At every turn objections were raised by civil libertarians and others who worried about the potential for government intrusion. Meanwhile, Latinos and some civil rights advocates complained that only foreign-looking people or those with unusual names would be subject to strict checks by employers, thereby creating a new type of discrimination. Finally, businesses fought any proposal that increased their exposure to legal penalties or that imposed greater personnel costs. All along the line proposals for identity verification systems died as employer sanctions were debated; in the ten years since the law's enactment, the same ideas have come back again and again only to be shot down by the same confluence of political forces.

By the time employer sanctions became law in 1986, a laundry list of documents, including many that were easily counterfeited, had been approved for use by people seeking jobs. The demands on employers had been scaled back so that they would not be faced with a heavy administrative load, and huge loopholes were created for employers who complained that they had made an honest mistake in hiring an illegal alien. Moreover, Congress failed to create an enforcement mechanism even for these loose rules.

The plan was to rely on voluntary compliance, and most diligent employers did comply. These, of course, are the same employers that routinely check the identity of a new hire, pay the proper withholding and social security taxes, and are most likely to keep safe workplaces, pay good wages, and offer medical insurance. The law shut illegal aliens out of these workplaces unless they could come up with very good false papers. But the rest of the labor market remained open to them, and illegals readily found work with employers willing to break the law, first of all by hiring them and then often by violating many other rules designed to keep jobs safe and fair.

While the immigrant influx gained momentum and permanence, the government made no credible effort to seek out and punish employers who continued to hire illegal aliens. Having enacted the 1986 law after years of contentious debate and deal making, Congress acted as if the problem were solved and moved on to other concerns without providing the resources or political will needed to make the new law effective. Between 1989 and 1994, the number of INS agents assigned to the enforcement of employer sanctions dropped by half, as did the number of fines issued. Despite an illegal population estimated at 4 million, the INS completed only 1,761 cases producing fines against employers in 1994. Meanwhile it accumulated a backlog of 36,000 leads on possible violations that had never been investigated.[9]

So illegal immigrants kept coming, and they kept finding jobs with people willing to break the law. Nobody stopped them, and nobody punished their employers.

Meanwhile, the temptations to hire illegals mounted. The rapid expansion of service industries, intense competition among national chains in areas like food service and retailing, global competition in many areas of manufacturing, and regular economic downturns have all helped create a broad sector of the economy that employs large numbers of low-wage workers and that operates on thin profit margins. Paying overtime under such circumstances can mean the difference between profits and bankruptcy.

Employers in this sector are under intense economic pressure to reduce costs by breaking workplace laws, and there is no countervailing pressure from law enforcement obliging them to follow the rules. Labor Department inspectors reported that only 47 percent of the workplaces they visited were in full compliance with the rules on verifying the immigration status of new hires. Most often these workplaces violated many other rules as well. For example, in the California garment industry, which is heavily dependent on the work of illegal aliens, a 1994 Labor Department survey found that nearly 93 percent of manufacturers violated health and safety rules, 68 percent failed to pay proper overtime, and half did not pay their workers the minimum wage.[10]

Although the illegal flows ebbed for a couple of years after the enactment of employer sanctions, this was a temporary phenomenon that lasted only long enough for potential migrants to realize that no serious obstacles had been erected in their path. Along the border south of San Diego, migrants massed in groups of several hundred every night to move into the United States unopposed. The Border Patrol complained that it was understaffed and underequipped but received none of the extra funding it was promised when employer sanctions were enacted. By the early 1990s, Americans seemingly had grown to accept the presence of illegal aliens and their widespread employment in illegitimate jobs. On both sides of the border it became apparent that the 1986 law had failed to deal with the problem decisively, and indeed its failure made illegal immigration a more permanent fixture. The fact that this behavior continued even after Congress had acted loudly to prohibit it only reinforced the idea that with a wink and a nod illegal aliens received permission to live and work in the United States.

Then, in the mid-1990s, the American people decided again that this problem needed to be fixed, just as they had in the 1980s and the 1970s. But when people began looking for new policy responses, their search was hampered by the legacy of ambivalence. The best options had been wasted. Current law lacked credibility, and illegal immigration had become more deeply ingrained in American society. The traffic was uncontrolled. And many citizens were angry.

CHAPTER 4

DRAWING LINES IN THE LAW BOOKS

Anyone walking along a downtown street in a major American city in the mid-1990s would find it impossible to distinguish accurately which of the passersby were native-born Americans, which were legal immigrants, and which were illegal immigrants. The nation's urban population is a mixture of all three, and immigration or citizenship status is not something people wear on their sleeves. In the climate of anxiety created by the backlash, the temptation among many people is to assume that anyone foreign-looking is in fact a foreigner. And if that person looks poor and Hispanic, the assumption is that he or she is probably illegal.

During a time of large-scale immigration, there is a tendency in the host society to define foreign-looking people simply by their apparent "otherness" and to deal with them as a single mass, ever more threatening because of their agglomeration. This reaction is by no means unique to the United States or to the 1990s. It is the classic nativist response to immigration, and it is as old as human wandering on the face of the globe. Leaving aside the moral and cultural questions raised by nativism, the temptation to see all foreign-looking people as a single alien mass poses some very distinct problems for policymakers.

In the midst of a mature migration, the nation has a large population who arrived as immigrants but are now citizens. There is also a growing number of U.S.-born children of immigrant parents. Finally, there are many people who share the same ethnic heritage as newly arrived immigrants but who are in fact native minority groups with long histories here, principally Hispanic and Asian Americans.

As a result of these complexities, the decisionmaking process must avoid creating situations in which people will suffer discrimination simply because they seem foreign. At the insistence of Latino and Asian advocates, this was a major concern in the development of the employer sanctions legislation adopted in 1986, and it has remained a controversial point in any proposal that requires people to verify their identities in order to separate out illegal aliens. The concern is that employers, or school and hospital administrators in the case of Proposition 187, will ask only foreign-looking people to verify their identity status or, worse yet, that employers simply will not give jobs to those who look foreign in order to avoid the risk of punishment for hiring an illegal alien.

The danger of increasing discrimination must be addressed every time the scope or severity of enforcement actions against illegal immigration is extended. This danger is especially great when the initial enforcement action—the decision not to accept an applicant for a job or a public benefit—is in the hands of an ordinary civilian, such as a foreman or a school secretary, who is not a trained law enforcement officer.

Other problems arise when policymakers attempt to deal with illegal aliens and legal immigrants at the same time. These two populations involve different challenges and require different responses. Until recently, the two realms had been kept separate in policy discussions. The Hesburgh Commission implicitly linked the two in its recommendation to close the "back door" of illegal immigration so as to better open the "front door" of legal immigration. But, from the start, the implementation of this plan was envisioned as two very separate legislative projects. The 1986 law dealt with illegal aliens, and the 1990 law dealt with legal immigration.

The wall between these two policy realms broke down in the backlash of the 1990s. In 1995, the House Judiciary Committee produced a single, sweeping bill that proposed measures to deal with both illegal and legal immigration, while in the Senate, Alan Simpson wrote two bills with the intent of marrying them together later.

The danger of mixing together policies for illegal and legal immigration is that neither will be addressed effectively. The two areas involve contradictory goals and conflicting methodologies. One is meant to punish and deter illegal activities. The other is meant to regulate and encourage a legal, even desirable human ambition. In one case the nation is trying to keep trespassers off its property. In the other, it is drawing up a guest list for a gala.

And, as with all unlawful activities, society must accept that it will be impossible to eliminate all illegal immigration. Much can be done, but after a certain point the law of diminishing returns sets in. As such, every immigration policy initiative should be subject to a cost/benefit analysis that measures both its actual costs and its impact on the quality of American society. Government could reduce illegal drug use more substantially with a much greater investment of funds, but this would require diverting money from other priorities. It also could take actions like universal random drug testing, but this would put a burden on all citizens and infringe on their civil liberties. Any effort to combat illegal immigration faces the same limitations.

Legal immigration requires a completely different outlook and set of tools. It more nearly resembles a regulatory activity, like the management of national forests or control of the money supply. The goal is to direct the use of an important resource, legal immigrants, in a way that serves the interests of our nation and that provides the greatest benefits possible for both the immigrants and the society that receives them.

Illegal immigration requires policies that are clear, sharp, and statutory, and a willingness to deal with the dangers of unintended consequences. Legal immigration requires policies that are flexible and dynamic, and a willingness to cope with the difficulties of trying to mold a huge demographic event to conform with national interests.

As different as they are, these two realms of immigration policy must be coordinated not only with each other but also with polices in seemingly unrelated areas that are deeply affected by immigration. Chapters 5 and 6 offer some suggestions on how immigration policy in these two areas might develop.

CHAPTER 5

ILLEGAL IMMIGRATION POLICY:
THE RUSH FOR AN ANSWER

T he immigration backlash of the mid-1990s must be considered a protest against the failures of past immigration policies
more than simply a reaction to increased immigration flows. If the
backlash can be given a precise starting point, it might be the day
in July 1993 when Governor Pete Wilson of California sent an
open letter to President Clinton in the form of a full-page adver-
tisement published in several newspapers around the nation. "We
can no longer allow compassion to override reason," wrote Wilson.
He insisted that the cost of providing public services to illegal aliens
was bankrupting his state. He argued that the nation's traditions of
keeping an open door to foreigners should not overshadow the
need for decisive action on illegal immigration. He accused the
federal government of failing to control illegal immigration and
demanded bolder steps.

As is often the case when advocates want attention for their
issues, Wilson reached for that ultimate remedy, a constitutional
amendment. He proposed altering the terms for gaining U.S. citizenship so that the children of illegal aliens would no longer be eligible simply by virtue of birth in the United States. Proposing a
constitutional amendment of any sort is more a political statement
than an act of policymaking. The primary intent is usually to convey

a sense of urgency rather than suggest a practical course of action. New crises do not generate calls for constitutional amendments. Old ones do. Wilson's proposal in the summer of 1993 captured the widespread feeling of frustration with all previous measures to combat illegal immigration and illustrates the context created by two decades of ambivalent and unsuccessful policymaking.

When all else seems to have failed, the political impulse is to find a large and sweeping measure that will solve the problem all at once. This is the impulse that propelled Wilson and inspired the Proposition 187 campaign in 1994. The fact that the measure was unconstitutional on its face and would provoke a legal battle all the way to the Supreme Court did not dissuade proponents—rather, it excited them.

The same desire for a coup de grace lay behind many of the proposals drafted in Congress in 1995. When the House Judiciary Committee voted to double the size of the Border Patrol in five years, it did not matter that this was a practical impossibility. Take a force of five thousand agents, add a thousand more a year for five years, and you've got ten thousand people on the border. The math was so exquisitely simple that it proved politically irresistible. It didn't matter how many experts argued that the Border Patrol was institutionally incapable of training, equipping, or supervising so much additional staff in so short a time. Under political circumstances such as those created by the immigration backlash, the grandeur of a proposal can be more important than its consequences. (This is not to deny the importance of the border, which had been grossly neglected by Congress and several successive administrations. Some semblance of effectiveness has been restored only since 1994; what is necessary now is a long-term program of institutional development within the Border Patrol that emphasizes improved leadership, better pay, and a higher-quality force— not just more staff.)

Few areas of national policy lend themselves to grand gestures, and immigration, legal or illegal, is no exception. The problem with grand gestures, aside from the fact that they rarely accomplish their aims, is that they produce a plethora of unintended consequences. Despite the conventional view of immigration as a discrete issue, it is firmly linked to several other important policy areas. Immigration policy involves law enforcement, economic regulation, and foreign policy. Because of this, sweeping plans aimed at resolving immigration problems can have huge repercussions in the areas of civil liberties, living standards, and international relations. The temptation is to move quickly and decisively, but immigration is precisely the kind of policy area that requires gradual, consistent, and incremental action. Even when deciding seemingly isolated questions, such as family preference visa numbers, it is essential to search out their broader implications. This is most apparent when it comes to plans to combat illegal immigration.

PROPORTIONALITY AND LINKAGE

Illegal aliens constitute less than 2 percent of the entire U.S. population. Yet several of the most frequently cited proposals to eliminate the illegal flow would affect directly the lives of all Americans and potentially change the very nature of American society.

The most common proposals to make employer sanctions an effective weapon against illegal immigration would require every employer to check the identity of a job applicant with a government agency before that person could be hired. These proposals generally involve the creation of a computer registry that would contain files on everyone in the country eligible to work, regardless of nationality. An employer would have to check prospective workers against the registry before they could be employed. And, of course, the only way to make such a system fair is to demand such a check for all hires—not just those involving presumed foreigners. Some proponents of a registry, such as the Commission on Immigration Reform, have suggested that it could also be used to prevent illegal aliens from utilizing public health, welfare, or education services. If enacted, this proposal would require that every resident of the United States, citizen and noncitizen alike, be registered from cradle to grave and that permission from the registry be sought for everything from enrolling in a community college course to signing up for meals on wheels.[11]

But a registry alone would not be enough to halt the employment of illegal aliens. Even if an employer were obliged to ask a prospective hire for a Social Security number and birth date and then check that information against the computer registry, there would be no certainty that the data belonged to the person standing in the employer's office. The data could still be bought or stolen. So most of the proposals also include some kind of verification scheme, such as a "counterfeit-proof" Social Security card that would include a picture and fingerprint, as well as the kind of physical information (height, weight, and so on) found on a driver's license.

Such proposals raise many issues, two of the most important being proportionality and linkage. As with all policy decisions, it is important to consider whether the solution is commensurate with the problem. In this case it seems that the illness is neither so extensive nor so severe as to merit the cure being proposed. Also, it is important to ask what precedents a registry and verification system might create for government action in other policy realms. Would this form of worksite enforcement have implications in areas like the collection of payroll taxes, enforcement of child support orders, or the maintenance of credit records?

Proportionality and linkage must also be kept in mind when considering other proposed solutions for illegal immigration. For example, to contend with the sudden influx of a large number of aliens, such as the Cuban rafters in summer 1994, the Clinton administration and others have proposed enabling the federal government to declare an immigration "emergency," which would allow it to suspend certain constitutional guarantees and normal legal procedures. Once such an emergency is declared, people entering the country would no longer have full recourse to the constitutional rights—such as habeas corpus, protection against self-incrimination, or the right of appeal—normally granted to anyone in the United States. Although proponents insist that the proceedings would be fair, they do not disguise the fact that the goal would be to enable the government either to intern or deport aliens quickly and efficiently, without going through the standard procedures involved in applications for political asylum or deportation orders. If the government had preauthorized capabilities to suspend constitutional guarantees in immigration emergencies, what is to stop it from seeking the same capabilities to deal with other kinds of situations? Even if intentions are honorable and there is no immediate threat to civil liberties, one must ask whether the dangers involved merit compromising basic principles of American law.

The same question arises with proposals for a constitutional amendment to bar the children of illegals from becoming citizens. Surely there are some people who enter the country illegally with the idea that someday they may have children and that they would like those children to be U.S. citizens. (Since a considerable majority of illegal aliens are single males, this group may not be large.)

The question is whether it is worth tinkering with a constitutional provision that reflects our basic philosophy of nationhood and citizenship in order to remove one reason for coming to the United States illegally.

Given these very basic concerns, there is good reason to postpone any serious discussion of such sweeping proposals and ask first whether there are other options that involve more limited forms of action with less potential for collateral damage. The answer quite clearly is that there are such options, but they have not been given due consideration in the political atmosphere created by the backlash. Many of these options involve making better use of existing policy tools and investing in long-term and gradual solutions.

PICKING A BATTLEFIELD

Since fighting illegal immigration is at its core a law enforcement issue, one of the first matters to be decided is where to focus activity so that it has the maximum effect on potential violators and the minimum impact on those who are uninvolved or innocent. Choosing every workplace in the country as a venue for enforcement actions against illegal immigration guarantees a substantial impact on many tens of millions of workers and employers who will never have any dealings with an illegal alien. Similarly, a requirement to check the immigration status of the parents of every child enrolling in every public school would put a new administrative burden on millions of school administrators who have never had an illegal alien in their classrooms.

What are the alternatives? As a start, enforcement efforts should be concentrated outside the country and at its borders and ports of entry, rather than in its workplaces, welfare offices, schools, and hospitals. The idea is to work from the outside in, to concentrate enforcement efforts first in those places where they will affect the fewest Americans and then consider other options. An interagency report on alien smuggling delivered to the White House at the end of 1995 concluded that far greater efforts could be made to ensure the cooperation of foreign governments in combating this trafficking in human beings. Having succeeded in getting the Colombian government to assist in an assault on the Cali drug cartel, Washington policymakers would have good reason to assume that the government of Guatemala can be persuaded, cajoled, and assisted in fighting the alien smugglers who have made that country a major transit point. Similarly, in dealing with Russia and several Eastern European states, cooperation and effective action on this score could be made a precondition for receiving U.S. aid and trade privileges.

This would not be a peripheral action. High stakes are involved. The interagency report estimated that 100,000 people a year from outside the region pass through Central America on their way to the United States, mostly from Asia, along with an estimated 200,000 to 300,000 from Latin America. Meanwhile Russia and Eastern Europe are hosting as many as half a million illegal immigrants who are trying to get to Western Europe or the United States. Yet, while Congress proposed beginning work on a highly speculative and intrusive computer registry of workers in 1995, it denied an INS request for additional personnel to be used in overseas antismuggling operations. (By juggling some resources internally, the Clinton administration has managed to add a mere fifteen agents to the effort.) Aside from citing a dire need for additional resources, the report noted that alien smuggling is not even a crime in many countries and is punished only lightly in others—yet the United States has just begun pressing foreign governments for changes in these laws.

Before policymakers consider measures that will have a considerable impact on the American people in their daily lives, they must do all they can to halt smuggling at its source and in countries through which immigrants travel. Whenever drastic measures are proposed, the first question should be: "Have we tried everything else?" The answer right now is "no" for a long list of possibilities.

A great deal can be done even within the parameters of existing congressional proposals. A thousand new agents a year may be too many to add to the Border Patrol, but they also could be used for antismuggling investigations here and abroad, greater enforcement at airports here and abroad, and more investigations of businesses such as the garment industry that traditionally employ illegal immigrants.

Moreover, a variety of measures can be taken to combat illegal immigration by people who enter the country as tourists or by other legal means and then stay and work illegally. Consular offices overseas are woefully understaffed and ill-equipped. No system is in place to keep track of whether or not people leave the country when they are supposed to. Resolving these deficiencies is simply a matter of allocating resources. Bar code technology or other forms of data management could be employed so that the United States would know when someone overstayed a visa. (If Wal-Mart can track its inventory, the United States certainly can track its visitors.) It would not be necessary to hunt down and deport those who overstay. Rather, the goal would be to pose a credible threat that if an alien overstayed a visa, it would be the last time he or she would enter the United States, and, moreover, it would be very unlikely that any of the alien's immediate family would ever receive any kind of visa.

More complicated problems arise from the growing number of Western European countries that are exempt from visa requirements for short stays. All that anyone needs to pass through a U.S. airport unchallenged is a good forgery of a French or British passport. This will become an increasingly attractive open door if the United States succeeds in blocking other avenues of illegal entry. The trade-off here is that the Europeans would respond in kind if the United States imposed visa requirements. But if illegal immigration is such an important issue that it is worth considering a constitutional amendment redefining the nature of American citizenship, then it is worth imposing some formalities on people traveling across the Atlantic.

All these issues need to be addressed methodically and with a considerable commitment of resources before the government can justifiably resort to such drastic measures as a constitutional amendment or a computer registry program. If lesser measures are tried and illegal immigration is still considered a grave danger, then it will be appropriate to discuss intrusive solutions—but not before then.

PICKING A FORUM

The commission headed by the late Barbara Jordan may have opened a Pandora's box with its embrace of technology as the answer to illegal immigration, but there is no reason to assume that the idea of creating a federal computer registry of workers is going to disappear even if everyone agrees that there is other work to be done first. The concept of linkage becomes especially important in this context. Such a registry and the identity card that would go with it will never be an instrument of immigration policy alone and should not be discussed primarily in an immigration context.

The overriding issues raised by this proposal involve the uses and abuses of information about individuals. Should the government collect such information in a centralized place? How should it be stored? Who should have access to it and for what reasons? As it becomes increasingly easy to gather and manipulate information about the entire population, these questions cannot be avoided.

The nation must decide whether it wants to have a federal computer registry, but that discussion should center on the potential conflict between high technology and civil liberties. Illegal immigration need be no more than a footnote in this discussion. This is but one example of how deliberation over immigration policy needs to proceed with an acute awareness of how it is linked to entirely different and potentially more important issues. The ongoing debate over legal immigration offers other examples of such linkage.

CHAPTER 6

LEGAL IMMIGRATION POLICY: REGULATIONS, NOT REVOLTS

G iven the degree of attention focused on illegal aliens it is easy to forget that two or three times as many foreign-born people come to live in the United States every year by following the rules. The persistence of illegal immigration, the government's failure to address it effectively, and the resulting backlash have all contributed to a law enforcement mentality that pervades the entire system. The experience of recent years has only heightened the presumption of guilt directed at anyone trying to immigrate. This is not just a matter of attitude; it is a problem that lies at the very core of the nation's immigration system.

Although its intent is to distribute a precious benefit—the right to live and work in the United States—the immigration system is designed to stop the wrong people from getting in rather than ensuring that visas go to the most worthy. Immigration laws, enforced by the Department of Justice, determine who immigrates with the same kind of rigid moralism normally associated with the punishment of crimes. Applicants need to fit into immigration preference categories that are defined by statute as precisely as any felony. These categories come with their own system of numerical caps instead of sentencing guidelines. And, like commandments of a different sort, immigration laws seem to be written in stone.

Instead of being handed down on a mountain, immigration laws traditionally have emerged from lengthy deliberations and multivolume reports by presidential commissions. Then come years of legislative debate. Prior to the Immigration Act of 1990, the last major reform of the legal immigration system was enacted in 1965; before that the last big change had been in 1924. Logically enough, when Congress sets out to write legislation that is supposed to serve for a generation or more, the temptation is to produce big bills that deal with every contingency and that cover every aspect of policy. The major immigration bills drafted in both houses of Congress in 1995 are no different. Indeed, their sponsors touted the measures as vehicles for fundamental change that would substantially reduce legal immigration overall and also finally defeat illegal immigration. Such laws are meant to set a definitive direction for the entire immigration system all at once, and they leave little room for administrative maneuver.

Authoritative statements and permanent measures may be appropriate when dealing with unlawful activity such as illegal immigration, but this kind of policymaking is inherently flawed when it comes to the legal flow. Legal immigration does not require such large and long-standing measures. Under contemporary conditions, when the United States is trying to manage a mature migration that is already well under way, such regulatory structures are actually counterproductive.

Migratory flows are simply too unpredictable to assume that laws will perform as expected for decades at a time. The huge increase in immigration from Latin America and Asia since the 1965 law utterly defied the predictions of its sponsors, who marshalled a good deal of reasonable evidence to argue that just such an increase was unlikely. Conditions in the United States are equally variable. The framers of the 1990 act did not see that a recession was just around the corner, nor did they understand that the end of the cold war and a wave of corporate restructuring would change the demand for skilled workers in the U.S. economy.

In recent years the static legal immigration system has created dire problems for the United States, would-be immigrants, and their sponsors. Family members of immigrants in some categories face waiting lists that will take more than a decade to clear under the 1990 act. Businesses that want to sponsor a specific individual must go through a charade known as "labor certification" in which they prove that no similarly qualified individual is already available in the U.S. labor force. Such absurd conditions encourage illegal immigration, fraud, and a "beat the system" mentality both here and abroad. The best argument for a new look at the laws governing legal immigration is not that the flows are too large or that immigrants are harming the nation, but that the system has lost its credibility and much of its effectiveness. On that point one finds little disagreement from passionate restrictionists, immigration advocates, or people merely trying to make their way through the morass of regulations. What is entirely missing, however, is any consensus on the direction of a new policy.

Virtually all of the debate in the mid-1990s has been over the size of legal immigration. On that point there is never likely to be any strong consensus because there is simply no right answer. It is impossible to make a definitive case that the nation will be better off in the year 2004 admitting 550,000 legal immigrants, as the Jordan Commission proposed, or the 700,000 or so allowed under the 1990 act. Such numbers can be debated endlessly, and they will be even more subject to debate in 2004 than they are now. That is inevitable. But it poses a problem when policymakers try to construct an immigration system that is supposed to last for a decade or more. Rather than debate what should be the proper size of the immigration flow from now until well into the future, the first issue that should be addressed is the longevity of such calculations.

The experience of recent decades shows that the traditional form of long-term policymaking for legal immigration does not work. No one would suggest that interest rates be locked into place for long periods of time, yet the United States does this for legal immigration—an essential source of manpower with a large effect on the economy. No one would suggest that international trade be governed by a rigid system of preference categories and annual limits, but this is what the United States does with legal immigration—a form of international traffic that deeply influences relations among nations.

Instead of once-in-a-generation overhauls of the entire system, regular, small-scale adjustments could produce a migratory flow more responsive to the nation's needs, less subject to unintended consequences, and less likely to inspire the kind of backlash that has distorted consideration of the issue in the mid-1990s. In the long run both political and practical concerns are likely to push policymakers toward developing a system of legal immigration that is more flexible, more technical, and more focused on short-term objectives. The hallmark of such a system would be a statutory requirement that the numbers and the criteria for legal immigration be subject to periodic reexamination. This is not an entirely novel concept. The upper limit on refugee admissions is set every year through a consultative mechanism that brings together representatives of Congress and the executive branch. Something similar could be devised for family and economic immigration. An annual appraisal would be excessive, but a reexamination every four years timed to the start of a presidential term might be effective and would certainly guarantee that the issue got the attention it deserved.

These periodic reassessments would not call into question the basic principles of immigration policy—principles like seeking enrichment through diversity, offering safe haven to the oppressed, and allowing the family to serve as the chief mechanism for settling newcomers. The basic structure of legal immigration would remain intact. But the overall number of visas and their distribution among various categories of immigrants, as well as special initiatives and exceptions, would be reexamined on a regular basis. This would oblige policymakers to consider the composition of the immigrant flow and its impact on the nation, while considering how that flow can be manipulated to better serve national interests.

By reviewing the mechanics of legal immigration periodically, policymakers could deal with emerging issues before they become the kind of large-scale problems that promote a backlash and result in drastic solutions. For example, having perceived that migration has reached a point where a large number of parents are being sponsored for entry, the government could evaluate the situation systematically and in its full context. A demographic increase in the number of people eligible for any government benefit increases the potential for fraud. Instead of attacking the increase in elderly immigrants as a cause of fraud in the Medicaid and Supplemental Security Income programs, the first step would be to examine the provisions in those programs designed to combat fraud. Then the government could experiment with measures such as those proposed by the Jordan Commission, which would require the sponsors of elderly immigrants to provide enforceable affidavits of support. Knowing that the entire matter would be reviewed in a few years, policymakers would be more inclined to give these efforts a chance to succeed before resorting to the more drastic approach of eliminating immigrants' eligibility for key safety net programs, as in the Republican welfare reform plans.

The process of taking stock would in itself stimulate healthy changes in the structure of immigration policymaking, as well as in the policies themselves, without challenging basic principles. Congress traditionally has taken the lead in defining immigration policy, with the INS functioning almost purely as an administrative and enforcement agency with little role in policy development. A process of regular reassessment would oblige a change in this distribution of labor by requiring a more intense focus on immediate conditions both in the United States and in sending countries. This cannot be accomplished with long legislative deliberations and weak executive branch authority. Since Doris Meissner became INS commissioner under the Clinton administration, the agency has developed its capabilities considerably. In order to work with Congress in a process of regular consultation, the INS would have to evolve much further and Congress would have to relinquish some of its prerogatives. In order to deal with the full linkages between immigration and other realms of policy, the agency would have to develop a capacity to integrate its work with that of other executive branch agencies and departments. Rather than a set of immutable laws, the immigration system would evolve into a regulatory process as flexible and dynamic as the resource it is trying to manage.

The mechanics of such a system are less important than two basic principles: First, the visa numbers and selection criteria that are the guts of an immigration system need to be reassessed on a regular basis. Second, this reassessment needs to take place with an awareness of current trends in the immigration flow and an idea of how government can redirect them in order to achieve objectives not just in immigration but also in the many other policy areas with which it deals.

Both family and economic immigration offer illustrations of how the nation has been ill-served by policies that have remained static for too long.

FAMILY IMMIGRATION: ELIMINATING FALSE EXPECTATIONS

Families always have been the major vehicle of immigration to the United States either informally or more recently as a matter of law (see Table 6.1). This is widely regarded as an important reason for America's success as a nation of immigrants. Families provide the new immigrant with a reception committee and support network that assists in finding housing and work far more generously than any government agency possibly could. Moreover, families of all nationalities and cultures have proven extremely effective in helping new immigrants make the transition to the English language and to American ways. For these reasons, the 1990 law set limits for family immigration nearly four times higher than for economic admissions (meaning those sponsored by employers). Even some of the most restrictive proposals maintain the basic emphasis on family while trying to bring down the overall number of immigrants.

Immigration law traditionally has defined a ladder of categories based both on the closeness of the relationship between the applicant and the sponsor and on the sponsor's status (that is, citizen as opposed to legal permanent resident). No numerical limits are placed on applicants with the strongest claims: the spouses, minor children, and parents of U.S. citizens. They are allowed into

TABLE 6.1
MAJOR CATEGORIES OF LEGAL IMMIGRATION

Category	Numerical Limits	1996 Projected Use
Family admissions	480,000	480,000
Employment admissions	140,000	100,000
Refugees	varies each year	90,000
Diversity	55,000	55,000
Total	———	725,000

Source: U.S. Commission on Immigration Reform.

the country as legal permanent residents, meaning they can live and work here for a lifetime and eventually become citizens themselves. All other potential family immigrants are ranked in a hierarchy of preferences. For example, the adult unmarried children of U.S. citizens get a higher ranking than the relatives of legal permanent residents. The total number of family immigrants is subject to an overall cap, with the allocation among preference categories decided according to complex formulas (see Table 6.2).

Despite its apparent logic, this system fails families by creating unfulfilled expectations. The law establishes visa categories for certain types of relatives but does not grant nearly enough visas to meet the demand. Under the law, someone who has just entered the country as a legal permanent resident, the basic form of legal immigration, has the right to sponsor a spouse and minor children as legal immigrants. But once the application is filed, those relatives go to the end of a waiting list of more than one million people. Because the law creates overall limits on the number of legal immigrants who can come from any single country, the waiting times

TABLE 6.2
MAJOR CATEGORIES OF FAMILY IMMIGRATION

Categories	1994 Usage
Unlimited	
Spouses and minor children of U.S. citizens	193,394
Parents of U.S. citizens	56,370
First Preference	
Adult unmarried sons/daughters of U.S. citizens	13,181
Second Preference	
Spouses, minor children, adult unmarried sons/daughters of legal permanent residents	115,000
Third Preference	
Adult married sons/daughters of U.S. citizens	22,191
Fourth Preference	
Brothers and sisters of U.S. citizens	61,589
Total	461,725

Source: U.S. Commission on Immigration Reform.

are longest for immigrants from countries that have the greatest number of people already here and who are generating the largest number of family sponsors. So, for example, there is more than a forty-year wait for the siblings of U.S. citizens seeking immigrant visas from the Philippines and a twenty-year wait for those from India and Mexico.

This is an exceptionally dangerous situation in the midst of a mature migration. Instead of spending a lifetime on a waiting list, people from all over the world make their way to the United States either illegally or on some kind of temporary visa, then remain here as illegal aliens with the help of their relatives. Not surprisingly, the greatest numbers of perpetrators come from countries with the most immigrants already in the United States, meaning those with the longest waiting lists.

Once this pattern becomes apparent, U.S. consular officials in the problem countries naturally become more cautious and suspicious when they are asked to issue visas for temporary visits to the United States. A young Filipino or Pole who does not own property or a business that ties him or her to home will find it very difficult to get a visa to the United States, especially if the purpose of the trip is to visit relatives here. In the end the system becomes self-defeating. It does not engender family reunification but rather becomes a barrier to it. It does not facilitate legal immigration but rather guarantees a steady flow of illegal traffic, particularly from nations that already have a large number of legal immigrants inside the United States.

An immigration system responsive to current conditions could preserve the family as a central vehicle for legal immigration while taking account of the fact that the United States is now dealing with a mature migration. Nearly three decades of accelerating family-based migration have created powerful and effective channels that draw newcomers to the United States. Those who favor tight restrictions refer to this as "daisy-chain" immigration. However one values it, there is no doubt that family immigration is self-reproducing and can develop into a centrifugal and expansive force. One immigrant is admitted, marries, and the spouse is admitted. They become U.S. citizens and can petition for parents and siblings. These new immigrants can sponsor their spouses and children, and so on. The result is rapid escalation in the size of waiting lists.

Simply reducing the number of visas issued to family immigrants may not actually reduce the human flow. As noted above, the momentum of expectations is such that the power of family ties can and will overcome legal obstacles and produce illegal immigration when legal avenues are blocked. Now that this process is well under way, with new countries continually joining the list of nations that send substantial numbers of family immigrants, it becomes difficult—perhaps impossible—to realistically estimate its long-term potential. Currently, most of the immigration debate is focused on overall limits for family immigration. Instead, the focus should be on how to manage the very powerful migratory patterns created over the past three decades.

An immigration system built on a regulatory rather than a law enforcement model and one that requires regular reassessments might have a better chance of responding to this situation. The goal would be to allow the current momentum to play itself out while limiting the extent to which it encourages illegal immigration. This kind of effort would require much more flexibility and experimentation than is possible under a system built on long-standing statutes. Having operated a system that created family trees stretching all over the world, the United States could decide to spend a period of time—perhaps a few years or a decade—allowing these family channels to run their course. Some new sources of immigration would be desirable and inevitable, but the emphasis in the short term would be on tapping out existing sources.

The first step in this kind of initiative would be to declare that clearing the backlogs would take priority for some period of time. This would mean that no new applications would be accepted for a given visa category, or it might mean halting applications from countries with excessive waiting lists. Because these decisions would be temporary and would have to be reviewed after a fairly short time, they would not carry the weight of permanent pronouncements. This presumably would make such decisions more palatable to those who would see themselves as losing out.

The Commission on Immigration Reform made several recommendations aimed at dealing with the backlogs in its 1995 report on legal immigration. It suggested increasing the number of visas for the spouses and minor children of legal immigrants and eliminating other categories that are heavily oversubscribed, such as the siblings of U.S. citizens. Simply eliminating such categories has the advantage of disposing of a waiting list with a stroke of the pen, but policymakers would have to accept the likelihood that some substantial proportion of those 1.6 million brothers and sisters who have already applied for visas would end up here as illegal aliens. The commission's report was the first substantial effort to grapple with the policy implications of the family visa backlogs and could provide the basis for future work in this area.

One of the difficulties highlighted by the Jordan Commission is the extent to which the 1986 amnesties for illegal aliens are contributing to the backlog in legal immigration. Under the terms of those amnesties, some 2.76 million people became eligible for legal immigrant status and are now gradually becoming eligible for citizenship. Currently, the spouses and children of amnesty beneficiaries, totaling some 1.1 million immediate relatives of legal immigrants, account for about 80 percent of the backlog in their visa categories. The Jordan Commission recommended that these applicants be admitted only after others on the waiting lists whose sponsors initially entered the country by legal means. This suggests an important point.

The 1986 amnesties produced a massive bulge in overall legal immigration, accounting for more than 40 percent of legal admissions during the five years the program operated (1989–93). Given the nature of family migration, the amnesty beneficiaries and their relatives can be expected to produce a similar bulge that will roll through the system for a decade or more as they become U.S. citizens and then seek admission for parents and siblings. The Jordan Commission's argument that amnesty beneficiaries be treated differently in terms of sponsoring relatives seems logical on the face of it. Sponsorship is a privilege that the government bestows, not a right. As the commission noted, "Those legalized under [the 1986 amnesty] already have received special treatment in obtaining amnesty. To further reward their earlier illegal entry by giving equal or higher priority to the entry of their relatives sends the wrong message at a time in which the U.S. must obtain greater control over abuse of its immigration laws."

The commission suggested putting the relatives of amnesty beneficiaries at the bottom of the waiting list, below the spouses and children of legal residents. This concept could be expanded readily. Amnesty beneficiaries could be denied all sponsorship rights after their spouses and minor children are granted admission. That is to say, amnesty beneficiaries and their relatives would not be eligible to sponsor siblings and parents even after they became U.S. citizens. Immigration would be limited strictly to the immediate family of the beneficiaries so as not to produce new and expanding family trees from this large pool of potential sponsors whose initial entry was illegal.

In addition to tackling the backlog, a regulatory-style system of immigration could undertake a number of other actions to manage the flow with temporary measures. For example, it could declare a hiatus in the granting of what are known as "post entry relationships" for legal permanent residents. At present, a person can gain immigrant status and then immediately marry and sponsor his or her spouse for immigration, as well as any children that are born of the marriage. Change would mean that no sponsorship privileges would be available for that marriage unless the immigrant became a U.S. citizen. The country also could create new forms of priorities for a period of time, such as declaring that family immigrants with a working knowledge of English or with postsecondary education would get favored places on the visa lists.

The major objective of this proposal is not to raise or lower the overall number of family immigrants in the short term but to increase the number of tools that policymakers have available to manage that flow. The unavoidable consequence of past policies is that there are already many more applicants than the nation is prepared to accept. That situation will prevail for another decade or more, and without intervention the level of unfulfilled expectations will only grow. Dealing with the backlog while reducing new applications in order to stem future growth would probably mean that the numbers would remain stable in the near term but that some of the pressures for greater immigration might be reduced in the long term.

Again, the final numerical results are less important than taking steps toward an immigration system that is responsive to current conditions and real needs rather than one based on legal abstractions and numerical targets. The need for such a change is also evident in the area of economic immigration.

ECONOMIC IMMIGRATION: SEEKING FLEXIBILITY AND LINKAGE

Like the system of preference categories for family immigration, the basic structure of economic immigration was developed decades ago. It took shape when, among other things, the United States had not experienced much immigration for thirty years and was not expecting much of an increase. Moreover it was a time when the

U.S. economy was overwhelmingly industrial and oriented toward the domestic market, where it was unchallenged by foreign imports. Needless to say, this situation has changed even while economic immigration has not.

Since 1992 an annual limit of 140,000 visas has been set for employment-based immigrants under five preference categories (see Table 6.3). That limit has never been reached (in 1995 only 83,000 visas were issued). The chief selection mechanism is "labor certification"—an infamous bureaucratic procedure administered by the Department of Labor through which an employer is asked to demonstrate, first, that no U.S. workers are qualified and available for the job that the applicant will fill and, second, that employment of the immigrant will not adversely affect U.S. workers.

After a two-year study of skilled immigration, the Carnegie Endowment for International Peace concluded that "the system is both unable to ensure that businesses have access to needed workers or to protect the interests of U.S. workers. The whole system invites manipulation and abuse." This is not the first judgment of

TABLE 6.3
MAJOR CATEGORIES OF
EMPLOYMENT-BASED IMMIGRATION

CATEGORIES	1994 USAGE
First Preference Aliens of extraordinary ability, outstanding researchers, Inter-nation executives and managers and their families	21,053
Second Preference Professionals with advanced degrees and their families	14,432
Third Preference Skilled workers (2 years training/experience)—professionals with baccalaureate degrees and their families	67,566
Unskilled workers and their families	9,390
Fourth Preference Ministers, their families, and other "special" immigrant workers	10,406
Investors	444
Total	**123, 291**

Source: Immigration and Naturalization Service.

its kind. Back in 1981, the Hesburgh Commission recommended scrapping the labor certification system, while the Jordan Commission reported in 1995 that "the only positive factor about labor certification that the Commission heard is that its cost (time and money) is a deterrent for all employers except those with the most pressing need."

To replace certification the Jordan Commission offered another form of labor market test in which employers would still have to demonstrate that they had tried to find a U.S. worker to fill the job and that the salary offered to the prospective immigrant was 5 percent above prevailing wages. In addition, the commission's plan would require employers to pay a "substantial fee" to support a private sector training program "dedicated to increasing the competitiveness of U.S. workers." Finally, the plan would make the resulting visa status conditional for two years, meaning that it could be removed if the immigrant were no longer working for the same employer at the same or a higher wage. In addition, the commission would eliminate employer sponsorship of unskilled workers, and at the other end of the spectrum it would exempt top managers and persons of extraordinary talent from any labor market test.[12]

The Carnegie Endowment recommends a much more radical change—a variation on the system used by Canada and Australia in which applicants receive "points" for certain desirable characteristics such as language ability, education, and skills. A great deal of fine-tuning would be possible under this system. The number of points granted for each characteristic and the total number necessary for admission could remain flexible. Points could be granted for people who had lived in the United States, who had previous professional experience in a given area, or who had attended school in the United States. The goal of such a system is to judge prospective economic immigrants not just by their qualifications for a specific job but rather as complete individuals. This stems from a recognition that although an immigrant may be admitted on the basis of a specific job offer, the visa granted is for a lifetime, and more often than not the immigrant will soon move on to other employment, sometimes in another occupation altogether.[13]

This recommendation points to an important change in the foundation of economic immigration. For a country with a highly technological, mobile, internationalized economy, filling a specific job slot should not be considered the major goal of economic immigration. Instead the goal should be to create a vehicle for importing human talent from other nations. Instead of concentrating on the first job that a prospective immigrant will hold during a lifetime in the United States, the focus should be on the individual, or rather the stream of individuals who would be enriching the country with their education and skills. Even though the applicant would still be sponsored by a specific employer, a point system could readily be manipulated with this broader goal in mind. And a point system would lend itself to the kind of regular reassessment and review that should be the basic mechanism for a reformed immigration system.

However, a system of economic immigration cannot be run merely as a beauty contest in which the most attractive applicants get the nod with no real consideration of their domestic impact. The labor certification system and other proposed reforms that remain focused on the immigrant's specific job description fall short because they are too narrow. Priorities for economic immigration should be set by examining conditions in an entire job niche, even in an entire industry or profession. The impact of economic immigration needs to be assessed not in terms of a single individual but with a realistic appreciation of the overall flow and its cumulative impact. This leads necessarily to an immigration policy deeply appreciative of its linkages to other policy areas. For example, thousands of foreign-born physicians and other health care providers have found employment in public hospitals both in inner cities and in rural areas. It is impossible to judge the desirability of this influx without examining Medicaid reimbursement policies and the pay structure of the health industry. In this case, as in others, the issue is not so much why employers are filling a given job niche with immigrants as it is why U.S. workers are not contesting that niche. Oftentimes they go elsewhere in search of better pay, leaving immigrants to fill whole job categories.

In other areas the problem extends even further to the question of why native-born students do not train sufficiently to fill certain professions. This is especially true in some engineering specialties and the hard sciences. The United States needs people in these fields, and immigration is filling the gaps. Economic immigration could readily be manipulated, particularly with a point system, so that the nation's graduate and professional schools become even more efficient conduits for a steady flow of the best and the brightest from around the world.

As desirable as this might seem, it is not the kind of strategy that can be developed in an immigration context alone. Instead, policymakers must examine the potential impact on U.S.-born students of having to compete against top students from around the world in order to gain admission to the best American universities. This is all the more a problem when the quality of graduate and postgraduate education in the United States remains among the highest in the world, while the primary and secondary systems that are charged with preparing students for those schools fall ever further behind.

The prevalence of immigrants in certain academic specialties is already a concern to some educators and advocates for U.S. students, especially those from minority groups. But as currently constituted, the mechanisms for developing immigration policy do not provide a way to judge these trade-offs. The problems are so complex and involve so many different types of policies and competing interests that they are unlikely to be resolved with a legislative bold stroke. Instead, the nation needs to recognize that this issue is going to be around for the foreseeable future and that it needs to be addressed through a process of incremental policymaking based on regular reviews and reassessments.

AFTERWORD

On Capitol Hill, the term *bell curve bill* has been coined to describe a kind of legislation that suffers an ever-narrower base of support the more it tries to accomplish. Some issues polarize Congress and the electorate to the degree that there are clearly defined voting blocs for and against the proposition. (Gun control and abortion are classic examples.) Immigration on the other hand is a bell curve issue where support falls off equally from left and right when a bold proposal is put forth. No real consensus forms either for or against modest immigration bills, but the bigger they are and the more they try to accomplish the harder they are to pass. Each additional provision loses two votes for every one it gains. This was the fate that befell efforts at sweeping immigration reform in both houses of Congress during 1995 and 1996.

As with several other major issues, Congress and the Clinton administration responded to widespread popular desires by proclaiming themselves in favor of bold changes in immigration policies, but they failed to find new mechanisms that would translate that political will into law. Instead, they revisited debates that date back to the 1970s in some cases, and generated more of the same ambivalence that has marked the immigration issue for nearly a quarter century. The same peculiar confluence of special interests emerged to confound policymakers, and as the proposals grew bolder, bigger, and more simplistic, support slipped away.

Regardless of its outcome, the 1996 election is unlikely to change this dynamic. From time to time immigration will flare up as a political issue. Declaring a commitment to combat illegal immigration more effectively has become an indisputable article of faith for presidential candidates, like the need to reduce the budget deficit. Broad statements about the need for a more effective legal immigration system will also be aired widely. But in the midst of the campaign season there are no signs of the kind of debate that might break the gridlock of ambivalence. Until the nation's leaders begin debating long-term strategies to deal with immigration, it is unlikely that much will be accomplished. Arguing the simplistic proposition of whether immigration is good or bad and then formulating simple proposals to either preserve or restrict the flow will lead nowhere. The bold promises and meager accomplishments of the 104th Congress are ample proof of this. Instead of looking for answers, the debate has to move on to murkier issues such as purposes and trade-offs, incremental measures, and consistency of effort.

Most of all, the debate needs to proceed from a recognition that a large-scale wave of immigration to the United States is already well-established and will continue for some considerable time. Policy formulated in the mid-1990s is policy formulated in the middle of an event. It is useless at this point to think about clean slates or fresh starts. Like it or not, America must prepare to take on the difficult and long-term task of managing a mature migration with a powerful momentum behind it.

To begin with, the public and policymakers should put away the thought that overall immigration flow can be reduced sharply over the course of a few years as was the case in the 1920s. Many restrictionists, both liberal and conservative, have proposed a return to so-called traditional levels of immigration, meaning those that existed during the fifty years between the end of the European wave and the beginning of the current wave. But such proposals ignore reality. Even if a law as drastic as the one that cut off immigration from Southern and Eastern Europe in 1924 could be enacted, it would prove impossible to enforce. Immigrants no longer arrive in the United States by way of long steamship voyages. Many come from close enough that they can walk or swim or take a leaky boat. Moreover, international travel has become a fixture of life even for people of modest means. Every year the United States records more than 300 million arrivals—by land, sea, or air—of those coming to visit for anything from a day to a lifetime. Decreeing a drastic reduction in legal immigration under such circumstances will result inevitably in an increase in illegal immigration. Enough of the flow is motivated by the powerful force of family reunification that it will not respond to simple restrictions.

The inescapable reality of managing a mature migration is that every action produces a reaction. Cutting off the flow of immigrant workers to certain niches of the economy causes jobs to move overseas or disappear. Reducing access to routine medical care for immigrants increases their use of emergency services. Adopting a broad definition of the nuclear family in order to satisfy the cultural traditions of certain well-established immigrant communities such as the Chinese means creating the circumstances for rapidly increasing immigrant flows from other countries that do not have a prior tradition of coming to the United States. Moreover, nothing changes quickly under such circumstances. Once an immigrant flow develops certain characteristics, it takes a long time to alter course.

This assessment is not meant to discourage initiatives to create an immigration system more responsive to America's needs. Rather, it is meant to reinforce the idea that the best long-term results will come from incremental, flexible efforts carried out over a long period of time—not through bold omnibus plans. The challenges of a mature migration did not develop overnight nor will they be resolved with a single law.

It took thirty years for immigration to the United States to develop the momentum that now lies behind it. During that time many people benefited from the labor of immigrants, and most people were indifferent to the flows. Policymakers settled for long debates and ambiguous results. Immigrant communities became well-established in every American city, linked to home countries by way of smoothly functioning human channels that bring a steady stream of newcomers to the United States. Millions of families have embarked on the move to a new country with the expectation that many of their relatives would eventually make the trip. And large sectors of the economy have become accustomed to, even dependent on, the immigrant flow.

Having created this situation, the United States will be living with it for better or worse for a long time to come. Much can be accomplished to redirect this flow to American purposes, and much needs to be done, but, to begin with, the public and policymakers alike must recognize that managing an enterprise of this kind will require many steps taken over many years.

NOTES

1. From the story of Barbara Coe as first recounted by the author in "California's SOS on Immigration; Initiative Would Cut Off Illegals' Benefits, Schooling," *Washington Post*, September 29, 1994, p. A.

2. Lyndon B. Johnson, Remarks on the implementation of the Immigration Act of 1965, July 1, 1968, Presidential Papers.

3. In this chapter, data on the immigrant population come from "The Foreign-Born Population: 1994," *Current Population Reports*, U.S. Census Bureau, August 1995, pp. 20–486. Data on immigrant flows come from *The 1994 Statistical Yearbook of the Immigration and Naturalization Service*, National Technical Information Service, February 1996, PB 96–113725. Data on immigrant population growth rates come from Michael Fix and Jeffrey S. Passel, *Immigration and Immigrants: Setting the Record Straight* (Washington, D.C.: The Urban Institute, 1994).

4. Philip L. Martin, "The United States: Benign Neglect towards Immigration," in Wayne A. Cornelius, Philip L. Martin, and James F. Hollifield, eds., *Controlling Immigration: A Global Perspective* (Stanford, Calif.: Stanford University Press, 1995).

5. John Bodnar, *The Transplanted: A History of Immigrants in Urban America* (Bloomington, Ind.: Indiana University Press, 1985).

6. The story of the raid on illegal aliens painting the Statue of Liberty appeared in the *New York Times*, January 10, 1975. The

plans of Immigration Commissioner Chapman appeared in the *New York Times*, September 22, 1974.

7. Doris Meissner's account of her conversation with Attorney General Levi comes from an interview with the author.

8. From Justice William F. Brennan, Jr.'s majority opinion in Plyler v. Doe, 102 S. Ct. 2382 (1982).

9. This account of INS enforcement efforts in the area of employer sanctions first appeared in the following article by the author: "INS 'Enforcement Deficit' Tied to Law; Voluntary Compliance Provision Fails to Deter Hiring of Illegals," *Washington Post*, February 2, 1995.

10. "Labor Abuse Rampant in State Garment Industry," *Los Angeles Times*, April 15, 1994.

11. For details, see U.S. Commission on Immigration Reform, "U.S. Immigration Policy: Restoring Credibility," Report to Congress, September 1994.

12. For details, see U.S. Commission on Immigration Reform, "Legal Immigration: Setting Priorities," Report to Congress, July 1995.

13. For details see Demetrios G. Papademtriou and Stephen Yale-Loehr, *Balancing Interests: Rethinking the Selection of Skilled Immigrants* (Washington, D.C.: Carnegie Endowment for International Peace, 1996).

INDEX

ABOUT THE AUTHOR

Roberto Suro was born and raised in Washington, D.C., the son of Hispanic immigrants. After graduating from Yale (B.A. 1973) and Columbia (M.S. Journalism 1974), he began a career as a newspaper reporter in Chicago. In 1978, he became a correspondent for *Time* magazine, eventually doing tours in its Chicago, Washington, Beirut, and Rome bureaus. From 1985 to 1993 he worked as bureau chief for the *New York Times*, first in Rome and then in Houston. He is now deputy national editor for the *Washington Post* and has completed a book on Latino immigration due to be published in 1997 by Alfred A. Knopf.